RETURN

Training Your Dog

Training Your Dog

DAVID KERR
DAILY MIRROR NATIONAL PETS CLUB

Illustrations by
JOHN ALLARD

David & Charles

Newton Abbot   London   Vancouver

British Library Cataloguing in Publication Data

Kerr, David
   Training your dog. — ('Mirror books).
   1.   Dogs — Training
   I. Title II. Series
   636.7'08'3   SF431
   ISBN 0-7153-7541-5

First published by Mirror Books Limited 1978
This David & Charles edition 1978
© Mirror Books Ltd 1978

Printed in Great Britain
by A. Wheaton & Co. Ltd., Exeter
for David & Charles (Publishers) Limited
Brunel House   Newton Abbot   Devon

Published in Canada
by Douglas David & Charles Limited
1875 Welch Street   North Vancouver   BC

Contents

Introduction

Why own a dog?

The great majority of dogs are kept purely as pets. A pet by definition is an animal kept for companionship.

Dogs perform a service to society that cannot be measured. They can be friends to young people, companions to the elderly, an aid to the handicapped and a comfort to the lonely.

A dog does not ask who or what you are. He does not care if you are a success or a failure, wealthy or poor. He simply repays your kindness and affection with unswerving loyalty. He can be your most uncritical friend.

Some people say that the companionship of their dogs is all that makes living worthwhile. Others believe a family is not complete unless they own a dog or a bitch.

Learning to respect and look after animals properly is a vital part of growing up. Psychologists believe pet ownership helps children become well adjusted, decent adults.

Owning a dog can give a youngster a sense of responsibility since the dog depends on him or her for food, proper grooming and exercise. This is the source of many lessons to be learnt.

The most basic lessons we learn from pets are about life itself. The expectation and arrival of a litter of puppies is a matter of tender curiosity to children and leads them to a natural understanding of birth.

Dogs grow up with children but grow old after ten years or so. The majority of dogs live out their lifespan between nine and eleven years. Their death is another lesson.

People who have lost the companionship of a much loved dog frequently say they will not have another and that no dog could ever replace their previous pet.

This is a shame. Not only does it deny them the pleasure of owning a dog but it is also denying a dog a good home. One dog does not replace another. They are all different in their ways and each is capable of winning its way separately into your heart. Each one will occupy a separate place in your memory.

Every year there are always many more mongrel puppies born than there are homes for them. Given a chance, they are just as capable of becoming good companions as pedigree pups.

There are plenty of other reasons for owning a dog.

They help you to meet people. Dogs are great ice breakers. Total strangers often start talking to each other because of their mutual interest in dogs.

More than a few dogs have played cupid by introducing couples in the park who otherwise might never have spoken.

Owning a dog helps its owner to keep fit. The dog demands to be taken out for regular exercise and the owner benefits too.

Dogs also work for us. Even the family pet instinctively acts as a guard, and a dog's presence is often sufficient to warn off would-be intruders.

Large dogs, such as Alsatians, Labradors and Dobermanns, are a very positive physical deterrent to burglars, but smaller dogs, particularly the terriers, are just as willing to have a go.

A dog can help capture a crook, and even the very smallest of all dogs, the tiny Chihuahuas and Yorkshire Terriers, still have the same highly developed instincts to guard and warn. What they may lack in size they can make up for in noise and so they are effective canine burglar alarms.

Dogs contribute to our society by working in jobs where their special qualities make them the tops.

Farmers would be lost without their working dogs, usually Border Collies, that help marshal cattle at milking time, or by rounding up sheep and by being watch dogs.

Armies and air forces use dogs for security work but

they have developed them to work in specialised roles.

Dogs, such as Labradors, with sensitive noses, are trained as sniffer dogs to detect explosives. It has been estimated that a dog's sense of smell is one thousand times more sensitive than our own, something almost impossible for us to imagine.

Dogs have been specially trained by mountain rescue teams to find missing people, possibly buried by avalanches.

A growing number of private commercial security organisations use dogs and those trained by police forces are a familiar sight.

Dog and police handler are trained to work together as a team. For general purpose police work, Alsatians are very popular. They have a strong deterrent effect on hooligans but are also used for tracking. Labradors have been trained to sniff out drugs.

Perhaps the greatest contribution dogs make is as

THE LADRADOR IS THE BREED MOST USED BY THE GUIDE DOGS FOR THE BLIND ASSOCIATION. BITCHES ARE PREFERRED TO MALE DOGS

AFTER FOUR TO FIVE MONTHS' TRAINING, THE DOG IS INTRODUCED TO THE FUTURE OWNER AND THEY UNDERGO A FURTHER MONTH'S TRAINING TOGETHER

GUIDE DOGS ARE CHOSEN FROM WORKING OR SPORTING BREEDS AND ENJOY DOING THEIR JOB. HOWEVER, WHEN THE HARNESS IS TAKEN OFF A GUIDE DOG IS AS FULL OF FUN AS ANY OTHER. SHE RETURNS TO DUTY AS SOON AS HER HARNESS IS PUT ON

guides to blind people. Guide dogs are carefully bred and selected for soundness, calm equitable temperament and intelligence.

The majority of dogs chosen for this work are Labradors but there are a number of Golden Retrievers and Alsatians. Some cross breeds are chosen also. The majority are neutered bitches.

The training of a guide dog brings out its best qualities but the dog's work does not end with being a guide.

In encouraging the blind handler to go out more often and further afield, that person's health benefits. He is able to go places and meet people, so his social life increases. For those who live alone, the guide dog is also a wonderful companion.

Dogs can sometimes help sick people overcome illness. People who could not venture out of the house have been helped over their fear of wide spaces by dogs that *need* to be taken out.

Withdrawn children may start to talk to a dog. Dogs that are happy and extrovert can have a beneficial effect on people who are withdrawn and unable to communicate.

Dog breeding, going to shows and obedience training are hobbies and recreational activities enjoyed by thousands.

There are now 150 different pedigree breeds recognised by the Kennel Club in Britain.

There are dogs which effectively do not bark, like the Basenji. There are others that do not need lots of exercise and some do not require a great deal of grooming. Some dogs have large appetites, others do not eat a great deal.

Some breeds, which include the members of the Spitz family, do not even have a doggy smell. Other examples are the Keeshond, Samoyed, Siberian Husky and Elkhound.

It is worth remembering that practically every breed was developed to suit a particular purpose. As a result, almost any requirement that you can think of for a dog can be catered for by carefully choosing the right breed in the first place.

The Breeds

Before we go into details about training your dog and looking after it—let's look at some of the breeds which are most popular in Britain.

Afghan Hound
An aloof, outdoor type that has become increasingly popular in recent years. This dog would be unhappy living in a small house or flat, where it would take up a lot of room. Affectionate with the family, they do not answer well to training and are suspicious of strangers. They have large appetites, plenty of energy to expend and demand a lot of hard work grooming them.

Alsatian
For years the Alsatian was Britain's most popular breed and even today only the Yorkshire Terrier is more popular. This large and intelligent dog needs firm handling and plenty to keep him occupied. Their coats grow better if kennelled outdoors. If kept indoors, moulting will be a problem. They are big eaters and need long walks and moderate but regular grooming.

Basset Hound
A sturdy, medium sized dog which is considered by some to be better as a pack animal than a pet. Their appetites are hearty and they have lots of energy. They require little grooming.

Beagle
Medium sized, pretty and popular as an agreeable family pet. Once voted Britain's 'canine dunce'. They do not train well but are full of energy and need lots of exercise every day. This surplus energy would be a trial in a small house or flat. Moderate appetite and the minimum of regular grooming is required.

Bedlington Terrier
The head shape and soft thick fleecy coat makes them look like lambs. The coat needs trimming but some people allergic to dog hair keep a Bedlington without trouble. A sporting terrier, they are hardy and love plenty of exercise and are generally good with children. Not expensive to feed.

Boxer
This breed has a reputation for making good and faithful family pets that get on well with children, although there are some exceptions that spoil this rule. Their short close coat requires only a few minutes attention every day. A moderate amount of exercise will keep them fit but some have large appetites.

Cairn Terrier
A small, hardy terrier with a wiry coat that demands little attention. They get on well with older children but can be snappy with little ones. They are typical fearless terriers. They do not need much exercise and require little food.

Cavalier King Charles Spaniel
Apart from the Yorkshire Terrier, King Charles are the most popular Toy breed. Intelligent and adaptable, they make good companions for all the family. As a larger Toy breed, they do not require a lot of exercise and are not expensive to feed. Nevertheless, their long coat demands plenty of attention every day.

Chihuahua
Rival to the Yorkshire Terrier for the title of our tiniest dog, the Chihuahua is intelligent and affectionate. Unhappily, some individuals tend to be delicate, vets say.

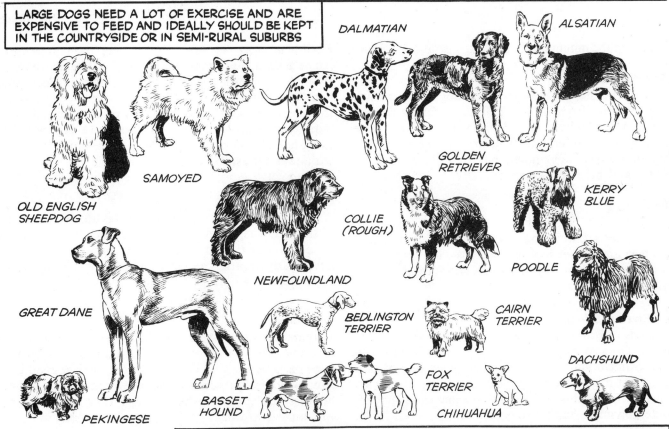

LARGE DOGS NEED A LOT OF EXERCISE AND ARE EXPENSIVE TO FEED AND IDEALLY SHOULD BE KEPT IN THE COUNTRYSIDE OR IN SEMI-RURAL SUBURBS

DALMATIAN

ALSATIAN

GOLDEN RETRIEVER

SAMOYED

OLD ENGLISH SHEEPDOG

KERRY BLUE

COLLIE (ROUGH)

POODLE

NEWFOUNDLAND

GREAT DANE

BEDLINGTON TERRIER

CAIRN TERRIER

DACHSHUND

FOX TERRIER

BASSET HOUND

CHIHUAHUA

PEKINGESE

EVEN SMALLER DOGS NEED REGULAR EXERCISE IF THEY ARE TO REMAIN HEALTHY

15

They require the minimum of food, exercise and grooming.

Cocker Spaniel
A tireless and happy medium sized dog that has won great popularity from its suitability as a family pet and companion for children. Train well if you take the trouble. Those long ears can be a problem, so keep an eye on them. Plenty of exercise is required but they have moderate appetites and need for grooming.

Collie (Rough)
Immortalised by Lassie of film fame, these Collies are intelligent and sensitive dogs. Medium sized, they require an average amount of food and exercise, but much more than average amount of daily attention to their soft, silky and profuse coats.

Cross Breed or Mongrel
Thousands of Britain's happy and contented pets have no pedigree. On size, appetite or energy, you will be taking pot luck unless you get the chance to meet one or both parents, but there is nothing to say that mongrels are less intelligent than pedigree dogs and in some cases they are considerably more hardy and good fun.

Dachshund
An intelligent and game small dog, although some are inclined to be snappy with small children. Their long bodies and short legs mean vets see more of this breed for treatment for slipped discs than any other. Energetic, they require little grooming and do not have big appetites. Long-haired, Smooth-haired, Wire-haired and Miniature variations are available.

Dalmatian
A muscular, medium sized dog that it is almost impossible to tire out. They need a great deal of exercise and tend to have a will of their own, so require firm handling. They have hearty appetites and the minimum of regular grooming is necessary.

Fox Terrier
Wire-haired variety very popular. A smooth-haired type available. Easy to groom. Weigh around 18 lbs. so their appetite is not costly. They are bright, active, good companions and alert guard dogs. They come from a tough hunting background which means they are better off with an active owner.

Golden Retriever

This breed is very popular due to their kind disposition, especially with children. The wavy and feathery coat requires regular attention. Being a sizeable working dog, the Golden Retriever has a healthy appetite. They are very intelligent and it is best to keep them active with plenty of long walks.

Great Dane

A dog that grows almost to the size of a small pony, but which for the most part is well mannered and intelligent. They are good with children, since being large they shake off any knocks which the kids might give them. They require little grooming and relatively little exercise. Although they do not have voracious appetites, being so large they are nevertheless very expensive to feed.

Jack Russell Terrier

This small, hardy, short coated or wire-haired terrier type is not recognised as a pedigree animal by the Kennel Club, so they cannot compete in championship shows. They are nevertheless very popular, spirited companions that are easy to keep and economical to feed. They need plenty of exercise.

Kerry Blue Terrier

Slightly larger than many terriers, this dog has a reputation for being a good guard and for becoming attached to the family. They require an average amount of food, grooming and exercise.

Labrador Retriever

A steady, hardy and reliable dog often seen working as a guide to the blind. They are obedient, easy to handle and get on well with children. They are large to have about the home, can moult profusely but otherwise need only a regular brush each day. They have hearty appetites.

Newfoundland

A really big breed, some weigh as much as a man. Coat is medium length, thick, oily, weather resistant and usually black. They love water and have made a name as canine lifeguards. You will have your work cut out to feed adequately, groom and exercise one of these giants.

Old English Sheepdog

Popular as a big, roly-poly playmate with families. Good with children and even-tempered. They have the disadvantages of taking up a lot of room, needing plenty of

T.Y.D.—B

exercise, having big appetites and their long, shaggy coats that require plenty of attention to keep in order.

Pekingese
Popular as companions, but perhaps better suited to older people or families with grown-up children. Coat requires a lot of attention. Not expensive to feed and only require moderate exercise.

Poodles (Miniature and Toy)
Intelligent, affectionate and enjoy company. The Toy is twice as popular as the Miniature and is easier to keep, exercise, feed and groom.

Samoyed
Typical of the Spitz breeds which include the Keeshond, Siberian Husky and Elkhound. They have no doggy smell. They are strong and energetic and have hearty appetites. The profuse, white coat of the Samoyed means plenty of grooming.

Yorkshire Terrier
Top of Britain's canine pops. This neat little terrier is both pretty and brainy. They make good house dogs but being tiny and easily trodden on, may be easily on the defensive when children are about. They have the tiniest appetites and need little exercise, but plenty of grooming is necessary to keep their silky coats in good order.

Choosing Your Pet

Because dogs are frequently chosen as family pets and grow up with young children people often ask which breeds are good with youngsters.

Here we must generalise, as there are good or bad examples in virtually every breed.

Bull Terriers, Labradors and Boxers have a reputation for being good with children, but some of the best dogs are mongrels and they come in all sizes and shapes. Most are good tempered, affectionate and lots of fun.

Every year, thousands of mongrels are put to sleep by animal welfare organisations and vets. If you want to offer one a home, contact your local police station, RSPCA or People's Dispensary for Sick Animals.

You can find them in the Yellow Pages telephone book. Look under the sections entitled 'Animal Welfare Societies' or 'Veterinary Surgeons and Veterinary Practitioners'.

When choosing a pedigree dog, it is important to find out as much as you can about the breed you have selected and the animal's temperament.

Throughout the year, there are hundreds of dog shows all over the country. At some, a variety of breeds will be shown, others may be one breed shows.

It is a good idea to go along to these shows and talk to

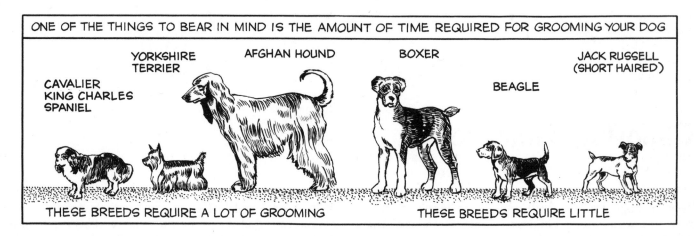

ONE OF THE THINGS TO BEAR IN MIND IS THE AMOUNT OF TIME REQUIRED FOR GROOMING YOUR DOG

CAVALIER KING CHARLES SPANIEL — YORKSHIRE TERRIER — AFGHAN HOUND — BOXER — BEAGLE — JACK RUSSELL (SHORT HAIRED)

THESE BREEDS REQUIRE A LOT OF GROOMING   THESE BREEDS REQUIRE LITTLE

the breeders. The more time and effort you put in at this stage, the less likely you are to regret your choice at a later date.

Advertisements for dog shows appear in local papers and in several dog newspapers and magazines which you will quite likely find at your local library. The Kennel Club will also be able to advise you.

An important factor that may narrow your choice of dog is the amount of grooming the animal needs.

Long-haired breeds will require up to 15 minutes thorough grooming, or more every day. Some heavy coated breeds, even though short-haired, tend to moult continuously.

If the dog's coat is light coloured and it lives indoors in a mild and comfortable environment, continual moulting and light coloured hairs everywhere can become a real problem.

It will be necessary to brush the animal vigorously

ten minutes every day to clean the coat, pull out dead hairs and tone up the circulation.

Some close or curly haired breeds have the reputation for hardly moulting at all. Poodles and Bedlington Terriers have sometimes been found to be suitable pets for people who are normally allergic to dog hair.

Owners of various pedigree dogs will disagree but there seems little doubt that some breeds are more intelligent than others. It is as well to recognise this before you embark on a training programme for your dog.

Given kindness and understanding most dogs, except the real tearaways, can be taught the elements of proper behaviour. Some breeds, like the Alsatian, seem gifted with a remarkable capacity for learning while others, like the Beagle, seem to lack brains.

Many Beagle owners quite readily admit that their pets must be among the canine world's dunces.

Puppy or Adult?

A further question you may ask yourself is whether or not to choose a puppy or try and obtain an adult dog.

Puppies are appealing but they bring with them the problems of puddles and housetraining. They need feeding up to four times a day when very young and often pass through an unruly stage elderly people cannot cope with.

If you are prepared to put up with this, then you will be able to bring up your pet from the very beginning in the way to please you.

Two to three months is the usual age to acquire a puppy. Smaller dogs tend to mature more quickly. Larger breeds mature more slowly and breeders will not let them go until they are a little older.

Older dogs are sometimes available from breeders who have kept a dog to assess its show potential. Animal welfare societies often have older dogs that need homes. Vets can sometimes help.

Each year the Retired Greyhound Trust finds homes for around 1000 ex-racing greyhounds (address page 125) but before you write to them for one, remember there are always plenty of people who are offering to take greyhounds and only a few of those applying will be successful.

Greyhounds are large dogs and need plenty of room and lots of food and exercise. An assurance is also required that the dog will never again be raced.

BY THE TIME A GREYHOUND IS FIVE YEARS OLD, HIS OR HER RACING CAREER IS OFTEN OVER – BUT THE NATURAL LIFE SPAN CAN BE FIFTEEN YEARS

EACH YEAR THE RETIRED GREYHOUND TRUST FINDS HOMES FOR ABOUT 1,000 EX-RACERS

GREYHOUNDS LOVE HUMAN COMPANY AND MAKE OBEDIENT PETS – THOUGH, AS WITH ANY LARGE DOG, IT IS UNWISE TO LEAVE ONE ALONE WITH A SMALL CHILD

A GREYHOUND NEEDS A LOT OF EXERCISE. HE OR SHE SHOULD ALWAYS BE KEPT ON A LEAD IN PUBLIC PLACES, OR THE RACING INSTINCT COULD CAUSE SERIOUS TROUBLE

The new owner must never forget that these greyhounds were born and bred and trained for racing.

To avoid accidents, the dogs must never be taken into a public place without being on a lead. This is not cruel, since greyhounds are trained on leads right from the word go. Moreover, they are adaptable and obedient.

They love the companionship of people and other dogs. After all, they are used to being in the bright lights and in the company of crowds of people and dogs.

They adore children, though, as with any large dog, it would be unwise to leave them unsupervised with small youngsters.

For most greyhounds, their sporting career at the top is fairly short.

By the time they are five years old, and sometimes sooner, they have given their best and are dropped from racing.

They could easily live until 15 but although owners are able to keep some, they cannot keep them all and that is why good homes are needed.

There is a certain amount of truth in the expression that it is difficult to teach an old dog new tricks; so if you do decide to adopt an older dog, remember it may have habits or vices that displease you. An older dog

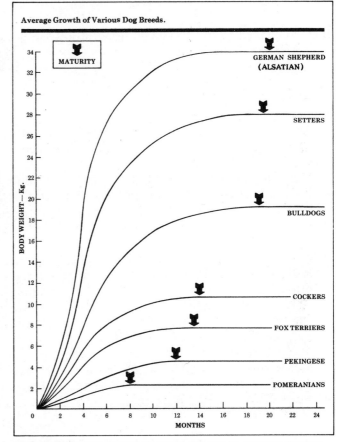

Average Growth of Various Dog Breeds.

GRAPH PREPARED BY PEDIGREE PETFOODS ANIMAL STUDIES CENTRE

23

that is not used to children could prove a problem if you have a young family.

Dog or Bitch?

Another choice you must make is whether or not to own a dog or a bitch. This is really a matter of personal preference.

By reputation bitches are often, though not always, more affectionate than dogs. They are sometimes cleaner and since they are inclined to be more willing to please than dogs, they sometimes respond more readily to training.

On the other hand, owning a bitch can be inconvenient since she will come into season approximately every six months after the age of five to eleven months, depending on the breed. Each season will last about three weeks, during which time you will have the perpetual problem of keeping her away from dogs, and dogs away from your door.

Bitches can be treated surgically by a vet to prevent them from breeding. This is called spaying. This will permanently stop them from coming into season but it is now an expensive operation. It can cost around £20 to £30, depending on the breed and where you live.

When a bitch is in season, she must be kept under control and constant supervision and not allowed to go out on her own.

There are proprietary preparations which may be bought to sprinkle on her coat to disguise the odour which attracts dogs. But these preparations neither prevent breeding nor deter every dog.

If a bitch does have an unwanted litter, this is not only inconvenient but can lead to the bigger problem of disposing of the puppies if you do not want them put to sleep and you do not have good homes already offered for them.

If a bitch is mated accidentally and you contact your local private veterinary surgeon quickly enough, it may be possible for the vet to give your bitch an injection to prevent her from becoming pregnant.

Today, there is a birth pill available for bitches which can be used to postpone her seasons at inconvenient times. A bitch will come back into season at a later date when the pill is no longer given and so can have puppies if you want her to. The effect of the spaying operation cannot be reversed.

If you choose to buy a dog, his sex will cause no trouble if he has sufficient exercise.

A dog's habit of cocking his leg against trees or lamp-posts is not merely to urinate but it is his way of marking out his territory. Bitches squat to urinate, so do puppies of either sex.

It is not advisable to put a family dog to stud as this can arouse instincts which are afterwards unwanted.

Buying Your Dog

It is quite easy to buy a dog. It is just as simple to take in a puppy or an older dog from one of the animal welfare societies. Ending up with the right dog to suit you, your family and your home, is a rather more difficult matter.

Today, dogs live longer because of improvements in their management, feeding and veterinary care. It is not so unusual for them to live into their teens.

Vets say that vaccinating dogs against distemper is largely responsible for this increase in their lifespans.

Choosing a dog then is not a task to be taken lightly since it may well be a member of your family for a considerable time.

You should first decide what size of dog you want. This will depend on three things—the size of your home, how much you can afford to spend on feeding your pet, and how much exercise you will be able to give him each day.

If you live in a town, smaller dogs are often the best bet. They will not take up too much house room, do not need a lot of exercise, and do not cost a lot to feed. About £2 per week is what you might expect to pay.

Larger dogs are best kept in the country. They will eat more than £4 worth of food in a week and you will need to take your dog for anything up to a seven mile walk every day to keep it fit and happy.

Needless to say big dogs are inclined to take up a lot of house room. Energetic breeds associated with sport and hunting often seem to take up a lot of room too!

When considering the size of your dog you need to consider if you are going to buy a pedigree animal or a mongrel.

It must be said that there are thousands of attractive, happy and intelligent cross-bred dogs. There has always been a debate whether or not mongrels are more intelligent than pure bred dogs, although no one has ever proved beyond doubt which of them is the more clever.

A ST. BERNARD IS NOT THE SORT OF DOG TO KEEP IN A TOWN FLAT. WHEN CHOOSING A PET, GO FOR ONE WHICH WILL SUIT YOUR HOME

THE HEIGHT OF THE ST. BERNARD IS ABOUT 28 INCHES AND THE WEIGHT 180-200 LB.

TOY BREEDS, LIKE THE POMERANIAN AND MALTESE, MAKE SPIRITED COMPANIONS—THOUGH TOY BREEDS ARE USUALLY WARY OF YOUNG CHILDREN

Mongrels are inexpensive to buy and you may even find someone willing to give you a cross-bred puppy if they know it is going to a good home.

On the other hand, it is possible to pay a lot of money for a pedigree dog. One that is a good 'show specimen' may be considerably more expensive to buy than an example of the same breed which does not measure up completely to show standards and so is sold at 'a pet price'.

In the last few years, there has been a swing in favour of buying pedigree dogs. Many dog experts, vets, animal welfare societies and even pet food manufacturers recommend buying such dogs.

The reason? Pedigree dogs are less likely to be misfits. If you know the breed, you know when you buy a puppy just how big and hairy it is going to become. Size and general temperament of the dog is already determined.

For this reason, if you choose a pure bred dog, you

can virtually match its temperament to your own. You will know fairly well if the breed's size and energy will fit into your home and life style.

The animal welfare societies feel there is a better chance that dogs chosen sensibly will remain agreeable family companions and not join the ranks of the canine un-wanteds. They also say that if people pay more for a pedigree dog they are likely to look after it better.

Unless you have a clear idea as to what both parents of a mongrel dog look like and you also know what their temperaments were, you can have no idea how a mongrel puppy will mature. How you both get on together depends more on pot luck.

Remember that all the pedigree dogs we see today were deliberately bred for a purpose. If you learn a little more about the history of a breed you are likely to buy, you may be able to spot any potential problems for yourself.

The Dalmatian is a good example. Many people see these dogs as being very attractive and about the right size. They have become more popular in recent years no doubt aided by their appearance in TV commercials and so on.

In the past, the Dalmatian was bred to run, first as guard, and then as decoration, behind stage coaches.

The result today is that as pets, they sometimes need firm handling as they have an inexhaustible supply of boundless energy. The result? Some people love their Dalmatians while other people are quickly worn out by them.

The breed will depend on what sort of life you want your pet to share.

If you are going to be taking long country walks in all weathers, then the Dalmatian, a Setter or one of the hounds will probably be just the dog for you.

Perhaps you want a working or shooting dog like a Springer or Retriever.

If you want a dog to act as a guard, then Alsatians and Dobermanns have the reputation for this.

If you want a guard dog but cannot afford to feed one of the larger breeds, then most of the terriers like the Kerry Blue, for example, have strong guarding instincts and will bark a warning of any intruder.

A Bull Mastiff or an Alsatian may represent a sizeable deterrent as a guard dog but if you live in a flat, all you may need is a small terrier or Pekingese which would act as an excellent burglar alarm.

If you live in a suburban house with a garden, you may

MONGREL OR PEDIGREE DOG?

MONGRELS ARE INEXPENSIVE TO BUY – YOU MAY EVEN BE GIVEN A PUPPY IN RETURN FOR A PROMISE TO PROVIDE A GOOD HOME FOR IT

PEDIGREE DOGS ARE EXPENSIVE, BUT MORE AND MORE PEOPLE PREFER THEM TO MONGRELS. THE BIG ADVANTAGE IS THAT YOU KNOW THE SIZE AND TEMPERAMENT OF THE PARTICULAR BREED

'MUTT'

YOU SHOULD TRY TO FIND OUT BOTH THE PARENTS OF A MONGREL PUPPY. THIS WILL GIVE YOU AN IDEA OF THE DOG'S EVENTUAL SIZE AND CHARACTER

IRISH SETTER

MONGRELS CAN BE HARDIER THAN PEDIGREE DOGS. SOME PEOPLE ARGUE THEY CAN BE MORE INTELLIGENT, BUT THIS CAN NEVER BE PROVED

settle for a larger dog, a Corgi, Spaniel or Labrador.

Generally speaking, Corgis are good, quick burglar alarms although somewhat impetuous.

Cocker Spaniels may seem slow but they are usually bolder and tougher than you would expect.

Labradors, especially black ones, have a tremendous psychological impact on an enemy.

If you live in the country an Alsatian may be the dog for you.

But remember, like people, dogs of the same breed can vary a lot. You can find a faint-hearted Alsatian or an aggressive but tiny Poodle.

Some people believe that the apple headed types, like Pekingese, Pugs, French Bulldogs and Griffon Bruxellois, are the most intelligent breeds, but it is the Alsatians and Border Collies that succeed so well in obedience and training trials.

You should choose the breeder or the supplier of your puppy with as much care as you choose your dog.

The names and addresses of breeders can be obtained from the Kennel Club or by scanning the weekly dog newspapers.

Undoubtedly the best way of deciding which breeder to visit is to follow the recommendations of friends or dog owners you know who have previously been pleased by the breeder.

You may well find that local vets will be able to provide you with the names and addresses of reliable breeders. They, after all, see the problems that result with puppies that come from unsatisfactory sources.

It is generally better to buy direct from a breeder who specialises in one or a few types of dog.

Puppies that are sold after passing through the hands of agents, shops and 'puppy farms', seem much more inclined to upsets. They are, of course, exposed to illness on their sometimes tortuous journey to the customer.

Puppies by mail order and sold on hire purchase terms, or that come from advertisers who offer every breed from Afghans, Airedales and Alsatians—right through the alphabet—often give disappointment. They can bring expense and heartbreak into a family rather than become the joyful companions they are intended to be.

You can learn a lot about a breeder if you arrange to visit his kennels or premises. If they will allow you to visit at other than a pre-arranged time, so much the better, since you will get a much more accurate impression of the way the establishment is generally managed, rather than see it put its best face on for visitors.

PUPPIES BY MAIL ORDER AND SOLD ON H.P. TERMS ARE SOMETHING OF A RISK. IT IS BETTER TO BUY DIRECT FROM A BREEDER WHO SPECIALISES IN ONE OR A FEW TYPES OF DOG

THE ENCLOSURES SHOULD INCLUDE A SHELTER FROM SUN AND RAIN, WITH A WOODEN PLATFORM FOR THE DOG TO LIE ON. RUNS SHOULD HAVE A HARD SURFACE

TRY TO VISIT THE KENNELS WITHOUT AN APPOINTMENT, TO GET AN IMPRESSION OF THE STANDARD OF MANAGEMENT

PERSONAL RECOMMENDATION BY A VET OR DOG OWNER IS THE BEST GUIDE TO KENNELS FOR BREEDING OR BOARDING

If you can, take a dog on approval or subject to a health check by your vet. If any kind of guarantee is offered, insist that it is in writing, dated and signed, and read the small print.

Now is the time also to make sure that you go away not only with the puppy, but with the precise details of its immunisation record to date and any pedigree papers.

If the dog is a pedigree and the breeder's declaration is signed at this stage, it will save you money if and when you wish to register it with the Kennel Club.

A good breeder should provide you not only with feeding instructions, but with information on how the puppy has been fed up to that time, plus some of the food the puppy is eating.

The reason for this is quite simple. The excitement of going to a new home, the journey there, and meeting new faces, is often enough to cause the puppy to have a digestive upset.

If you maintain the diet it is used to for a day or two then you will at least be deferring yet another change in the life of the puppy the day you take it home.

If you have consulted your vet about where to buy the puppy, you may have already made arrangements to have the animal examined. In any event, do this immediately, before any arrangement you have made with the breeder expires.

Points to Watch For

The following check list gives the points to watch for to ensure that you buy a healthy, good tempered pet since it is up to *you* to pick the right animal.

Trying to rectify mistakes afterwards can be a heartbreaking business with little or no financial recompense.

If you buy an unhealthy dog which you and others subsequently become attached to and it dies, you may find that you have little or no redress for your heartbreaking experience.

When you choose a puppy as a pet, remember that your own emotions and the way you look at life can affect him.

Find out as much as you can at the beginning about the puppy's background. Where and how was it reared and who looked after it?

These questions are most important if the heartbreak of choosing the wrong dog for you is to be avoided.

Show dogs are bred mainly for looks not temperament, so an impressive pedigree is not necessarily a guarantee of an ideal family pet.

BUY from a reputable source. Go to a breeder who has been recommended to you by other dog owners. Look the breeder, his premises and his animals over before deciding anything at all.

If you can see both parents of your puppy, so much the better as you will have a clearer idea of the temperament of their off-spring.

ASK an expert, perhaps a 'doggy' acquaintance or a friendly vet, to accompany you and be guided by their experience and advice. If you cannot have an expert go with you, then endeavour to take the dog on three days' approval, so giving you the opportunity to have the animal examined.

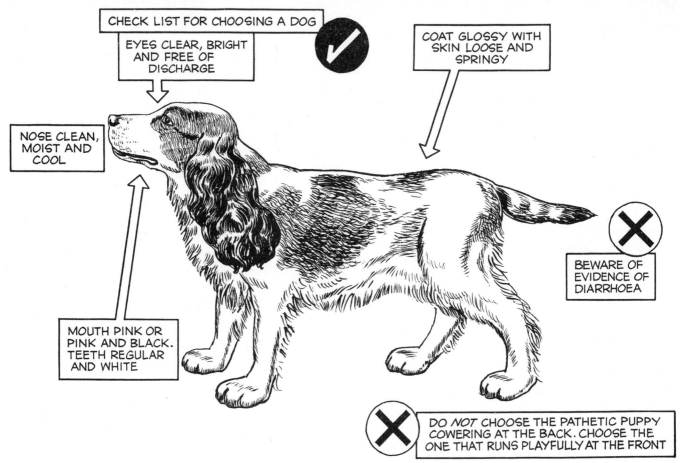

CHECK LIST FOR CHOOSING A DOG

EYES CLEAR, BRIGHT AND FREE OF DISCHARGE

COAT GLOSSY WITH SKIN LOOSE AND SPRINGY

NOSE CLEAN, MOIST AND COOL

MOUTH PINK OR PINK AND BLACK. TEETH REGULAR AND WHITE

BEWARE OF EVIDENCE OF DIARRHOEA

DO *NOT* CHOOSE THE PATHETIC PUPPY COWERING AT THE BACK. CHOOSE THE ONE THAT RUNS PLAYFULLY AT THE FRONT

Choosing Your Pet

BEFORE you buy, carry out this 'tip-to-tail' check of the puppy.

Nose — should be clean, moist and cool.
Eyes — should be clear, bright, alert and free of any discharge.
Mouth — lips, tongue and gums should be pink or a mixture of pink and black, and the breath sweet smelling.
Teeth — should be regular and white.
Coat — should be glossy and 'alive', with skin loose and springy. The coat around the tail should be clean and if any motions are visible in the kennel area, check that they are not loose. Buying a puppy with diarrhoea is buying a ticket to disaster. A healthy dog is always alert, inquisitive and playful.

It is very tempting, especially for young children, to want to take home the small, pathetic little puppy that cowers at the back of the kennel. Such a tiny mite is bound to arouse everyone's ptotective instincts and attract their sympathy. At this point you must be firm and make a

T.Y.D.—C

sensible decision.

It is the bold puppy that runs playfully to the front, shouldering his brothers and sisters aside and leaping up at you on his hind legs, that is most likely to make you the best companion. You are far less likely to be taking him or her on frequent expensive visits to your vet. Choose one of the nervous and dejected waifs of puppies you may find in kennels and you will regret it.

Settling the Puppy

The basic education of the small puppy cannot begin too soon.

The first lesson began on his first night when he had to contend with cold, hunger and loneliness for the first time. If he cried, he had started to learn the lesson that he cannot have all his own way.

Cold and hunger can be met by warm bedding and a small meal to last him through the night, but being alone is the thing he must get used to otherwise his owner will have no rest.

Some people say a ticking clock placed under the blankets in a pup's basket helps to give it a sense of security.

You should have prepared a warm, snug bed, a place he will come to know as his own, and on the first night he will learn to stay in it. On this point you must be firm.

The puppy will almost certainly cry during the night, missing for the first time the warmth and companionship of his brothers and sisters.

If, at this stage, you get up to comfort him or, worse, take him into your bedroom, then you will have started something the puppy will mean to continue.

His comfortable basket, a blanket covering a stone or metal hot water bottle, filled with very warm but not

SETTLE YOUR PUP IN FOR THE NIGHT— *NOT* IN YOUR BEDROOM
HAVE HIM EXAMINED BY A VET
Pedigree Certificate
REGISTER WITH THE KENNEL CLUB

boiling water, should be given to comfort him.

What You Need for Your Puppy

There are several items you are going to need in order to make your puppy comfortable and keep him properly.

Bedding

A must for your pup is a bed or basket to call its own. Give its choice some careful thought as this is an expensive item and should serve your pet for many years.

Although the price of baskets increases dramatically with size, get one that is going to be big enough for your pup when it becomes an adult. All too often, families buy an expensive basket which the pup rapidly outgrows.

There is a lot to be said for the traditional wicker baskets. They are cosy and comfortable. But it is unwise to provide your puppy with one until he has got over teething and chewing as wicker baskets are easily destroyed by a dog's pointed crushing teeth—and a great deal of litter is made in the process.

A stout cardboard box cut down to ease getting in and

out is the best proposition to start with. Place some old woollies in the bottom to make it snug.

There are framed folding beds which are convenient if you travel with your pet, but those which are covered and padded with fabric rather than washable plastic materials are more difficult to keep clean and hygienic.

Today, many breeders, kennels and dogs homes have opted for dog beds moulded in strong plastic or fibreglass. These are totally washable and hygienic and although the materials they are made from are cold, a blanket or bedding material which is easily washed or changed can be put in them to give the dog something warm to lie on.

It is possible to spend a lot of money on elaborate dog beds, some are even electrically heated, but for the average, energetic, outgoing family pet, this is likely to be a waste of money. After all, they do have fur coats and dogs were never designed to enjoy such luxuries.

Situating the Bed

The place where your dog's bed is going to be put needs just as much thought as the choice of the bed itself. A dog needs a corner or quiet spot to call his own. Somewhere he can retire to, to sleep peacefully, or where he can get out of the way when in disgrace, feeling off-colour, or simply fed up with being plagued by young children.

Ultimately, it must be a matter of personal choice if you are going to allow your dog to live indoors with the family or not. The majority of pet dogs in households today sleep in the kitchen, perhaps near a stove or central heating boiler.

As a result of this 'soft' indoor life, dogs' coats tend not to develop so naturally. But they are inclined to become more sociable and companionable members of the family.

There is really very little wrong with the idea of keeping a dog indoors, so long as the commonsense rules of hygiene are followed.

It is *not* a good idea to keep a dog in the immediate part of the home where food is prepared or eaten.

A dog that is kept out of doors in a cosy, dry, draught-proof kennel or outhouse, will probably develop a thicker, more weatherproof coat which is both insulating and rain-proof.

The same dog kept indoors in a possibly centrally heated dry environment may well moult throughout the year.

In the case of light coloured dogs, like yellow Labradors, a family can be driven to near desperation by the

EQUIPMENT FOR YOUR PUPPY

TOY

BASKET

LEAD

SLIP COLLAR

BRUSH

COLLAR

FOOD BOWL

WATER BOWL

DOG

COMB

NAME AND ADDRESS TAG

large quantities of hairs to be found over everything in spite of constant regular grooming to remove them each day from the dog. It is just one of the problems brought on by inviting the dog into the home.

Feeding Bowls

Your pet will need its own food and water bowls which should be washed up thoroughly every day, not with, but after any other washing up that is to be done.

It should be the rule in every home that the ideal bowl to buy is one that is heavy so that it will not skate around the floor when a dog tries to eat or drink from it. It should be shaped in such a way so that it is almost impossible to turn it over with nose or paw.

Bowls made from earthenware, heavy gauge stainless steel or thick tough plastic are ideal. Flimsy plastic or aluminium pots will not last long if a dog decides to get his teeth into the rim.

Collars and Leads

For the pup itself, you will need a sturdy collar with some means of engraving on it, or attaching to it, a tag with your name and address.

The law requires that every dog or bitch, when in the street or any other public place, must wear a collar with the owner's name and address written permanently on it. If everyone followed this simple and fundamental requirement there would be fewer stray dogs.

You will probably need to buy a small collar to start with. Make sure that it fits comfortably but is not so loose as to pass over the puppy's head when on the innermost hole.

At first, your puppy will probably resent wearing a collar so it is best to introduce him to the idea by making him wear it for a short while and gradually extending these times until he no longer fidgets to remove it.

Soon you will be able to attach the lead once he has got used to wearing the collar. Lead him short distances gently and he will soon get used to the idea that it is not a tug-of-war he will win. At first he will probably sit firmly down but be patient, encourage him with kind words and a walk will be a pleasure you both look forward to.

A word of advice about choosing suitable collars and leads. Avoid those made from flimsy plastic with a fabric backing and those which are held together with thin metal staples or tiny rivets. In no time at all, these collars and leads crack and split and suddenly your pet is free to run off, possibly at the most dangerous moment.

The best collars and leads are those made from good quality leather with all attachments like buckles and clips secured by heavy stitching.

Later in your pet's training, you may like to obtain a slip collar and a longer lead. If you are to become involved in advanced training, then a 45 ft. long line is needed for him to take part in tracking exercises.

Depending on the length of your pet's coat, you also need some basic items of grooming equipment. Suitable brushes and combs are available from the majority of reputable pet stores.

PUT DOWN NEWSPAPERS FOR THE PUPPY TO WET ON OVERNIGHT

USE AN ANTI-CHEWING SPRAY ON FURNITURE AND SLIPPERS AND HIS BASKET – LEAVE HIM ALONE AS LITTLE AS POSSIBLE – IF YOU DO LEAVE HIM, PUT HIM SOMEWHERE HE CAN DO LITTLE DAMAGE, LIKE A KITCHEN

Dog Licence

Do not forget once your pup reaches the age of six months you will need to have a current dog licence. People who have more than one dog need a separate licence for each.

The cost of the licence is $37\frac{1}{2}$p, an amount which has not changed for nearly 100 years, but general opinion considers this too low, so it may well increase at any time.

Application should be made at any post office or county or borough council offices. Dog licences must be renewed every twelve months and they are valid only in respect of the person to whom they are issued and cannot be transferred to anyone else.

There are some exceptions of dogs which do not need to be licenced. These include guide dogs used by the blind, and some dogs used only to round up sheep or cattle. Hounds less than a year old owned by hunts, but not hunted, are also exempt.

Incidentally, if you are caught without a dog licence, you can be fined £5 (or £20 if you claim exemption and you are not entitled to it). No one can escape being fined by taking out a licence the same day that they are caught without it.

If a person has been disqualified by a court from keeping

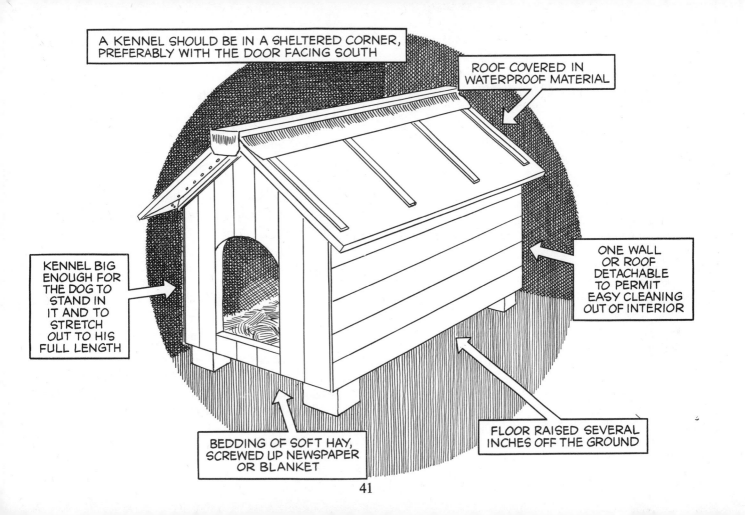

41

a dog, then it is an offence for him to apply for a licence for as long as that disqualification applies.

The person in whose name the licence is taken out should be the person who looks after the dog or keeps it in his house, unless it can clearly be proved to belong to someone else.

Your Dog's Kennel

The days when most dogs were kept in kennels, in the garden, now seem to be over. The present concept of the family dog is as a companion that shares your home and your hearth.

Working dogs, including police dogs, are kept out of doors the whole year round so that their coats develop fully and become wind and rainproof.

The construction of a kennel relates significantly to the dog's health and comfort. It is possible to buy kennels, but these can prove expensive items. They are constructed mainly from wood and they take a number of hours of skilled work to manufacture in comparatively small numbers. However, drawings and plans are available so it is possible to make the kennel yourself.

There are certain fundamental requirements that any kennel your dog occupies should meet.

1. The kennel must be roomy enough for the dog to stand and turn around easily or stretch out to his full length.

2. It should be situated in a sheltered location away from the prevailing wind and rain, preferably with the door facing south. It is more comfortable for the dog if the door is in the long side of the kennel.

3. The roof should slope and be covered with a completely waterproof material, such as asphalt sheeting or good quality linoleum.

4. The floor must be raised several inches off the ground. Water, leaves or rubbish must be removed before they get a chance to accumulate underneath.

5. At least one wall of the kennel should be detachable so that you have easy access for cleaning.

6. Soft hay, screwed up newspaper or a dry blanket should be provided as warm bedding. The interior of the kennel should be examined every day and properly cleaned and aired at least once a week.

First Things First

The first word your puppy must learn is his or her name. Whatever you do, do not choose a long and elaborate name for everyday use.

Such a name may seem distinguished, amusing or fitting when you bring your young scamp home and sit around the first evening trying to think of the ideal label. But remember, your pet may well be with you and the family for ten, twelve or more years. During that time you may have to shout that name hard and often in all manner of public places and any embarrassment aroused will be yours, not your dog's?

A short, sharp arresting name is one that will be learnt quickly by the puppy and will be most easily heard and appreciated at times when you demand it.

The next word your puppy must learn in basic training is NO.

You should only use this word when you really mean it and then ensure the puppy knows you mean it too.

Serious training should not begin until the puppy is around six months old. During the earlier months, his character will develop but that is not to say that meanwhile he should not learn to distinguish between right and wrong.

The fundamental principles of dog training are based on

producing associations of ideas.

Obedience to an order must be associated in your dog's mind with praise and reward. For a dog, kind words and a friendly pat are praise and reward enough.

It is not a good idea to base your approval of your dog's doing well on a succession of tiny tit-bits. They might make him eager but will also make him greedy and fat.

Disobedience your dog must learn to associate with scolding or, in extreme cases, a corrective slap.

If you are going about training your pet patiently and properly it should seldom, if ever, be necessary to hit him. Should you do so *never* kick or punch and never strike across the nose which is delicate and sensitive in a dog. A slap across the rump with a rolled newspaper makes plenty of noise without really hurting and should have the desired effect.

Although he will want to while he is teething, do not

let him chew objects indiscriminately. If you give him an old shoe to chew, you cannot expect him to tell the difference between that and the new pair you have just bought.

When trying to take objects away from your puppy however, do not get involved in a tug-of-war. Otherwise this is likely to be regarded as a game and he will resist you all the more.

Say NO in a harsh voice and gently prize the pup's mouth open by putting a finger between his jaws at the side of his mouth.

A stern word should be the only reprimand needed. It is far better and easier to cure your pup of bad habits when he is small. When he has grown much larger you can imagine that the damage he could do would increase proportionally and you may find it much more difficult to break irritating habits which have developed into vices in the older dog.

For example, puppies are inclined to rush at visitors and jump up at them in excitement however wet and muddy their paws might be. So it is never too soon to say NO and push them down firmly.

House Training
A young puppy has great difficulty in controlling his natural functions. But, as we note when talking about dogs' natural instincts, they are clean by nature and reluctant to soil their living quarters, so house training a puppy is not too difficult.

As soon as your pup shows the signs of wanting to relieve himself—wandering about and going into corners sniffing or squatting—you should pick him up and carry him outside. Leave him for a short while but make sure you give a warm welcome when he returns.

First Things First

Whatever you do, don't smack your puppy for wetting the carpet. Such punishment will frighten him and may delay the house training process.

NEVER rub his nose in his messes. This is an old idea which is both ineffective and cruel.

Your puppy is most likely to want to relieve himself after a meal or after a long sleep so put him outside immediately after he has eaten or woken up.

You must expect some accidents about the home; it is all part of having a puppy and watching it grow up. Put him outside immediately, and when you have cleaned up, disinfect around the spot where he made his mess so he does not associate the smell with a place to return to and do it again.

Out in the street a young dog should be taught to use the gutter when necessary. This is easier to teach if he is always hurried to the kerb every time he begins to slow down and look about him for an obvious reason.

It is not advisable to teach your puppy to make regular use of any small plot of grass since a grass patch may not always be available when the pup has to urinate or defecate. He may well feel that it is very wrong to go anywhere else. Using parks, recreation grounds and grassy play areas intended for children is unhygienic and makes

DOGS SIT UP AND BEG ALMOST BY INSTINCT — BUT DON'T FEED A DOG FROM THE TABLE...

IT MAY SEEM CUTE WHILE HE'S A PUP BUT LATER ON IT BECOMES JUST A NUISANCE

dog owners very unpopular with other local residents.

When your pet is a little older and is taken out for regular exercise, make these occasions after his meal times so that he will come to associate going out with being able to relieve himself. Make sure he does not go where he wishes but that you insist on his going to the kerb or gutter.

In many areas there are by-laws backed up by a fine for people who allow their pets to foul the pavement or public thoroughfares. You should take great care not to infringe these rules which are for everyone's benefit, including pet owners, so make sure you know what the local rules are and keep within them.

As dogs become old, it is sometimes less easy for them to control their functions. It is kinder therefore to divide their food into two or three separate meals a day, taking them out after each feed.

If an older dog wets or soils in the house at night time,

and sometimes younger dogs develop this habit too, feed them during the earlier part of the day and withdraw all water during the evening. Should the dog appear thirsty, then give it only an ice cube to lick before retiring for the night.

Teething Troubles

While still young your puppy may appear to be continually chewing. Don't imagine he is necessarily going to grow up to be utterly destructive, but remember that he is still going through the comparatively early stages of teething and is probably suffering some discomfort in the mouth.

Nevertheless, the puppy must not be allowed to indulge in destructive games, and biting and pulling things to pieces should all be stopped. In the same way, a puppy must not be teased by the children or it will tend to become snappy as a result.

Puppies are born without teeth and the temporary, or milk, teeth come through from three to five weeks old. The usual number is 28.

A puppy will start to lose the tiny pointed milk teeth at about three or four months although bigger breeds will teethe at a later date. Most dogs will have many of their full set of permanent teeth by the time they are five or six months old.

When you take your dog to the vet for routine vaccinations or if your pet seems to have difficulty eating, ask him to check the teeth. Sometimes a few milk teeth are not shed and cause problems when a permanent tooth erupts below them.

Any sort of pain in the mouth will tend to put a dog off his food and make him uncharacteristically grumpy and bad tempered. Most adult dogs have 42 permanent teeth.

T.Y.D.—D

Basic Training after Six Months

Why bother to train your dog beyond the first steps?

The answer quite simply is that it makes life a lot more enjoyable for you both.

The untrained dog will almost certainly be unhappy as a family pet. The reason is that without proper training, the dog will inevitably be in the wrong place and doing the wrong thing, according to you.

However you punish the dog, it is not going to know why it is being punished if it has not been taught right from wrong.

Having decided to get a dog and perhaps paid a lot of money for it, it is remarkable that thousands of people never bother to train it properly. But for these people, time is beginning to run out. In recent years a new awareness has developed concerning the responsibilities of pet owners.

Sadly, all dog owners can be affected by the misdeeds of the few.

If pets become unhappy, unhealthy nuisances, the chances are it is the owner who is at fault. Kept properly, dogs as companions can be a benefit to the whole community.

Uncontrolled dogs are likely to be a road safety hazard.

In an experiment in a busy urban area during which

REMEMBER THAT FROM THE DOG'S VIEWPOINT YOU LOOK HUGE, EVEN FRIGHTENING

ACT TOWARDS HIM WITH KINDNESS AND CONSIDERATION

JUST TAP HIM LIGHTLY IF HE MISBEHAVES – MERELY TALKING STERNLY TO HIM MAY BE SUFFICIENT

the laws concerning keeping dogs on leashes were strictly enforced, the number of accidents involving dogs was reduced to a quarter.

In Britain, the National Farmers Union claims that more than 10,000 farm animals are killed and injured by dogs each year. There must be many more instances that never get recorded.

A friendly and innocent looking dog can slip out of sight for five minutes and turn killer amongst farm livestock. Just chasing sheep for fun does the damage if the sheep are pregnant.

Ask anyone who really knows about dogs what is wrong with them and the chances are they will tell you, "There is no such animal as a bad dog, only a bad owner."

More people who do not own dogs would find it in their hearts to like them better if dog owners took the trouble to ensure that their pets did not cause a nuisance.

It is irresponsible owners who allow their dogs to roam the streets causing accidents, soiling the footpaths and worrying livestock. It is these owners who, without any doubt, fail to accept the responsibility of controlling their dog.

It is wrong to keep a dog that is going to be on its own for long periods every day. People who spend the larger

52

part of the working day away from home cannot expect to keep a happy and companionable dog. In these circumstances, it is often better that they do not have a dog at all.

If a dog is to be left alone for three or four hours each day, you could consider buying a second dog to act as a companion.

You must also consider your neighbours. Dogs that bark incessantly may irritate your neighbours to such an extent that they take legal action against you. Some owners are amazed to find that although a dog is quiet as a mouse while they are at home the dog barks continually as soon as they have gone.

It is a natural reaction for dogs to bark at strangers. You should immediately introduce a dog to visitors and say NO to his barking.

Earning Your Pet's Respect

It cannot be emphasised too often that a kind word and making a fuss of your dog with your hands, is of immense value.

If he is naughty or apparently disobedient, you should

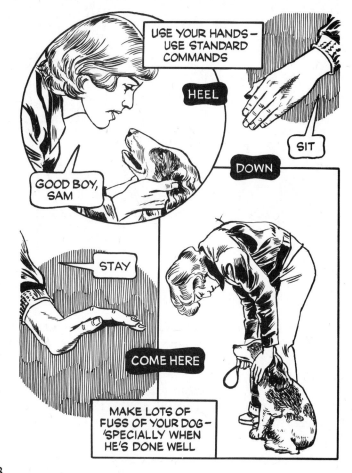

always bear in mind the fact that he may not understand what you have told him to do.

A dog does not learn the meaning of various words, he simply associates the sounds that you make and the actions that you take with actions that you want him to carry out.

You must always remain calm and patient and keep the lessons short, particularly at the beginning of his training.

It is better from the dog's point of view that one person is responsible for his training.

A well trained dog is happier than one that is completely spoilt.

Confidence in his master is half the battle in training a dog. He must learn that he can always trust you, and you in turn must never bully him. Bullying and shouting only produce complete confusion in the animal's mind.

It is useless punishing your pet long after the event.

A YOUNG DOG, LIKE A YOUNG CHILD, CAN ONLY CONCENTRATE FOR A LIMITED PERIOD. MAKE HIS LESSONS SHORT (BETWEEN 5 AND 10 MINUTES) AND FREQUENT

DO NOT WEAR ANYTHING THAT DANGLES OR FLAPS WHEN YOU BEND OVER HIM, FOR EXAMPLE A LONG NECKLACE OR SCARF OR AN UNBUTTONED COAT. THESE DISTRACT THE DOG'S ATTENTION

He will not be able to associate harsh words or being chastised with something he has done many minutes before.

We have said that if you are training your pet properly and patiently it should not be necessary to hit him. The occasional tap with a rolled newspaper will be all that is needed.

When dogs need correction for a misdemeanour, it is important that the scolding or punishment is given there and then.

After the event, he will not know why he is being punished and if you have called him to you first, he will be most reluctant to return to you again remembering the punishment that followed the first time.

In the early stages, any instruction you give your dog must be accompanied by a demonstration. When teaching your pet to sit, the word 'sit' should be spoken and his hind quarters should be firmly pressed down until he

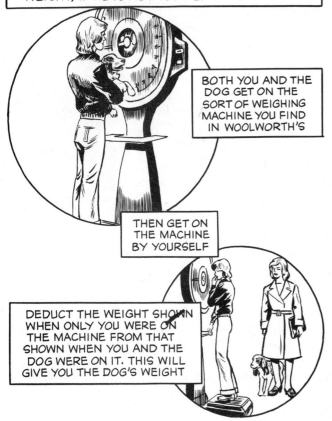

THIS IS AN EASY WAY TO CHECK YOUR DOG'S WEIGHT, IF HE IS NOT TOO HEAVY TO LIFT

BOTH YOU AND THE DOG GET ON THE SORT OF WEIGHING MACHINE YOU FIND IN WOOLWORTH'S

THEN GET ON THE MACHINE BY YOURSELF

DEDUCT THE WEIGHT SHOWN WHEN ONLY YOU WERE ON THE MACHINE FROM THAT SHOWN WHEN YOU AND THE DOG WERE ON IT. THIS WILL GIVE YOU THE DOG'S WEIGHT

takes up the desired position.

At first, he will immediately try to get up but the instruction should be repeated again and again and each time he should be pressed down until he sits properly.

As soon as he responds by staying in a sitting position for any length of time, this is the time for you to praise him with kind words and make a fuss of him with your hands.

No matter what you are training him to do, constant persuasion is required with firm repetition of the same word and the same action every time until the dog first begins to respond. That is the time for you to encourage him by making a fuss. Always use the same word to mean the same instruction. Do not say 'fetch' on one occasion and 'bring' on another.

It is impossible for a dog to concentrate for more than a few minutes, so do not bore him with long sessions of training. Five minutes at a time is often enough and ten minutes should be the limit of any training session you give him. The golden rule is to make his lessons short and frequent.

All training is based on an association of ideas. Take it gently and you will build up confidence between your pet and yourself.

'Heel' Sequence

Walking to heel is regarded by many as the first step in proper obedience training. A young puppy has nothing to gain from this exercise so do not attempt to make your pet walk to heel much before the age of six months. Some dogs will naturally come to heel and need no formal telling what to do.

By the time you teach your dog to walk to heel, he should be walking easily and naturally on a collar and lead. When walking properly to heel, your dog should walk steadily on your left, close to your leg but not in front of it.

The lead should be held firmly in the right hand, with a little slack. Step out on your right foot to walk at an even pace. If your pet attempts to forge ahead, correct him by sharply jerking back the head, simultaneously giving the order 'heel'.

When your pet walks properly to heel, praise him,

DOG IS SITTING FACING YOU

HEEL

RIGHT LEG BACK

DOG WALKS ROUND BACK

SIT

REPLACE RIGHT LEG

GOOD BOY, SAM

DOG SITS AT LEFT SIDE

but if he starts to wander off to one side, firmly order him to heel again, jerking the lead as you do so.

Should your pet be unwilling to maintain a steady walking pace alongside you, do not yank him forward using the collar and lead, but instead, stoop and pat the front of your left leg while still walking and talk to him encouragingly.

When your dog is walking to heel properly, allow the lead to go slack and he will quickly appreciate that wandering off in any other direction is going to result in your jerking him back into the correct position.

Once a dog is walking to heel properly, he should be able to follow naturally every change in your pace and direction and stop when you do.

Having encouraged your dog to walk naturally and comfortably to heel, you can allow him to walk this way without a collar and lead in any safe open space. But this first discipline you have taught him is NOT a substitute for walking with a collar and lead when in the street.

However well trained a dog might be, a momentary lapse in his discipline or concentration, caused perhaps by seeing a doggy pal across the street, may find him dashing out into the traffic. So at any time there is a risk from traffic, crowds of people or when among farm animals, your pet should be properly restrained on a collar and lead.

Using the Check Collar

A collar made from flattened chain links with a ring at either end, known as a check collar or slip collar (wrongly called a choke chain) is popularly used when obedience-training dogs.

Some experts and animal welfare societies frown on the use of this collar because it is all too easy for it to be put on the animal the wrong way round. If this is the case, once tightened, when the dog stops pulling, the chain does not naturally drop loose. So it is important to make sure *you* know once and for all which is the correct way round to fit the collar.

The illustrations show the correct way to place the check collar over a dog's head. There should always be sufficient slack for you to insert two or three fingers beneath it, but when the lead is jerked back the collar will tighten and the moment the lead is released the collar will fall slack again.

Fitting the collar the wrong way round can cause dis-

59

IF A DOG PERSISTS IN PULLING AHEAD, TURN ABOUT AND WALK BRISKLY IN THE OPPOSITE DIRECTION

IF HE PULLS AHEAD AGAIN, TURN ABOUT YET AGAIN. THE DOG WILL BECOME UNCERTAIN OF RUSHING AHEAD IN CASE HE IS LEFT BEHIND BY A SUDDEN REVERSAL OF DIRECTION

THOUGH YOU MAY FEEL A BIT SILLY DOING IT, REPEAT THE PROCEDURE EVERY TIME THE DOG PULLS AHEAD

tress and injury to the dog.

It is because so many people are inclined to fit the collar wrongly and others who follow their example get it wrong too, that the animal welfare societies are opposed to its use.

A check collar should never be used on a dog younger than six months old. Some large breeds are slow to mature and strengthen in the neck, so the chain should be used carefully and with discretion on such breeds until they are a few months older still.

The check collar will not necessarily stop a dog from pulling in front of you on his lead; a leather collar with buckle may do just as well.

One remedy for the dog that continually pulls ahead of you is for you to make a point of turning about and walking in the opposite direction each time he does it. You won't travel far to start with! But what will happen is the dog will be uncertain of rushing in front as he is none too sure that he will not suddenly become left behind.

Teaching Your Dog to 'Stay'

The next exercise you can progress to, the 'stay', should not be attempted until you are confident your pet has understood and thoroughly learnt the previous exercises.

At this point, your pet should fully understand and respond to the word 'sit'. He should also know exactly what you mean by NO.

Walk with him, on your left, stop and tell him to 'sit'. At this point he should be sitting on your left hand side. Turn and face your dog and say to him firmly 'sit and stay'. Repeat the order several times. At this point do not praise him or use his name.

If you walk backwards a few feet, your pet may attempt to follow. At the first sign of any movement say NO, point and take him back to the spot where you wish him to remain. Tell him again to 'sit'. Repeat the instruction to 'sit and stay'. When your pet has remained in the spot you have placed him for a quarter of a minute, then you can praise him. But if he moves before you wish him to, start the whole sequence again.

Repeat the lesson several times at regular intervals and increase the duration of the time you expect your pet to remain in the 'sit and stay' position. Only praise him while he remains seated. The moment he shows any sign

START WITH DOG SITTING AT LEFT SIDE

STAY — STEP FORWARD

STAY — FACE DOG

STAY — STEP AWAY

SAM, COME

SIT

GOOD BOY, SAM

END WITH DOG SITTING FACING YOU

YOU ALMOST CERTAINLY HAVE A DOG TRAINING CLUB OR SOCIETY IN YOUR LOCALITY. IT PROBABLY MEETS IN A HALL OR COMMUNITY CENTRE. SOME LOCAL EDUCATION AUTHORITIES AND ROAD SAFETY COMMITTEES ALSO RUN TRAINING COURSES

THE BASIC BEGINNER'S COURSE IS USUALLY OF SIX WEEKLY HALF-HOUR SESSIONS AND COVERS THINGS LIKE 'HEEL', 'SIT', 'DOWN', 'STAY', 'COME HERE'

CORGI

THE INSTRUCTOR WILL EMPHASISE THAT YOU CANNOT RELY ON THE COURSE SESSIONS ALONE AND THAT YOU MUST GIVE YOUR DOG A SPELL OF TRAINING EVERY DAY

of moving off, repeat the lesson and use the same actions and instructions.

As your pet's understanding of remaining in the 'stay' position increases and your control over him becomes more positive, you will be able to increase the distance that you can walk away from him.

This exercise must be repeated again and again at short intervals, day by day, until you are confident that your pet will remain where you have placed him and will

not move until you call him by name.

You should be able to increase the time when your pet remains seated to two or three minutes without difficulty but even after this time has elapsed, remember to make a great fuss of him when you return.

This lesson is particularly valuable. Although you should always have your dog on a collar and lead, in a situation where there are possible hazards arising from traffic or farm animals there can always come a time when

you and your pet are caught out. If he is away from you, you will, by word, be able to order him to 'sit and stay' and so keep out of trouble. So the lesson is one that your pet must learn thoroughly.

'Down' or 'Lie'

The next important exercise to teach your pet is for him to lie in the 'down' position when you tell him to.

A dog will assume this prone position when naturally at rest and its value to you is that when you instruct the dog 'down' he is switched off.

From this position, he is not likely to rush off and get into trouble or be a nuisance. Before he does anything he is going to sit up and that's when you put him 'down' again. While your pet is in the 'down' position, you are free partly from worrying about his next move, so you can

chat or carry on with whatever you are doing.

Begin by telling your dog to 'sit', on your left side, holding the lead short in your right hand. Tell him 'down' and pull down on his collar and lead.

If he is reluctant to assume a prone position, use your left hand to press down on his shoulders. Crouch down beside your pet and make a fuss of him WHEN he has done what you want him to.

After you have practised this routine for five or ten minutes every day for a week, you should be able to slowly stand up and your pet remain where he has been placed.

Making Your Dog Come to You. The 'Recall' Sequence
By now, your pet should 'sit' and 'stay' on your instruction.

For this training exercise you will need a long cord, a clothes-line will do. Attach the cord to your dog's collar and having told your pet to sit on your left side, tell him 'wait', and walk very slowly away in front of him paying out the line as you go. Make no sudden movements and do not use your pet's name. If your pet moves, you must both start again.

When you are several yards away, pause for a moment, then pull the cord gently towards you saying 'come'. Almost certainly he will readily want to join you. Remember to make a fuss of your pet when he comes back to you and show him where to sit and stay.

You should be able, after a number of short lessons, to increase the distances that you walk away from him and the time that elapses before you tell him to 'come'.

Perfecting this exercise is important because you never know where you will be or under what circumstances you may wish your pet to return quickly to your side and out of harm's way. You do not want there ever to be any likelihood of him disobeying you and running off.

You must have seen other dog owners made to look foolish. There they are in the park urgently calling their pets to come back to them. Their dogs, probably joined by others, are cheerfully running around apparently totally deaf to their owners' desperate pleas.

A Word of Advice

Once you have established the basic commands you may wish to go in for more advanced training. This is dealt with later on (see p. 71). But if you are happy with your dog and your dog is happy with you, be contented and thankful that you now have an animal that will be your life-long friend, if you continue to treat it properly.

Some owners think it clever to teach their dogs tricks. It isn't. It is degrading to both the animals and to the owners. Circus dogs dressed up in human clothes, performing 'funny' tricks may be amusing to watch and give pleasure to some, but how much better it would be if *all* dog owners treated their pets with the love and respect that the dogs are happy to give to their owners.

Dog Training Clubs

Thousands of Britain's young dogs go to school.

T.Y.D.—E

THE WELSH SHEEPDOG AND COLLIE ARE HIGHLY TRAINED. THEY ARE INDISPENSABLE TO THE HILL AND MOORLAND FARMER FOR ROUNDING UP AND GUIDING SHEEP, OFTEN ON UNFENCED LAND

THE SHEEPDOG TRIALS GIVE MEN AND DOGS THE CHANCE TO DISPLAY THEIR CLOSE PARTNERSHIP

THE OLD ENGLISH SHEEPDOG IS RARELY USED AS A WORKING DOG NOWADAYS

There are more than 500 dog training societies registered with Britain's Kennel Club (address page 125).

The number of obedience classes rises steadily each year—a clear indication that more and more dog owners want to make their pets socially acceptable.

Almost every town and district in Britain has a club where owners can take their dogs for obedience lessons.

The clubs usually meet on one or two evenings every week in school and church halls or community centres. Most charge a small weekly fee to cover the cost of the hall.

Some clubs have a basic membership fee and then make a small charge for each session. Others ask for nominal fees by the term.

The instructors are all experts in obedience work with dogs. In many cases, they have trained and won prizes with their own obedient champions.

The experts agree that serious obedience lessons should not be started until a puppy is at least six months old. But as we have already seen, a puppy can still be taught right from wrong.

It does not matter whether your dog is good or naughty, a brilliant pupil or just a dunce, he will almost certainly benefit from attending training classes and you will learn too.

For many distressed owners of delinquent dogs, their best course of action is to take their pets to training school where he will receive tuition from experienced dog handlers and be taught to behave well and obey commands.

Details of your nearest schools will be found in pet columns of local newspapers and veterinary surgeries.

A minimum of six lessons is considered necessary to complete a beginner's course, and if your pet does well you may like to enter for the advanced class. Explain to the instructor the difficulty you are having and he will study your pet's personality and advise you on the best way to handle him.

A dog that is unable to tell right from wrong and so is therefore often in trouble with his owner for no good reason as far as he can tell, quickly becomes a bewildered and unhappy animal.

Obedience lessons can be of benefit to dogs that are over a year old but remember, it is more difficult for older dogs to learn new ways.

In addition to dog training clubs and societies, there are also a number of evening classes run by area education authorities or sponsored by local road safety committees.

Local training clubs are well attended and some even

have waiting lists—evidence of dog owners taking their responsibilities seriously.

Although sessions only take place on one or two evenings a week you will be pleasantly surprised at the progress you and your dog make. The great advantage of attending these sessions is you can learn by seeing the mistakes other folk make. Moreover, your own mistakes are quickly spotted and corrected under the expert eye of the instructor.

Showing Your Dog

Almost everyone who owns a pedigree dog or bitch at some time thinks about entering his pet in a dog show. It is usually a neighbour, relative or friend who claims to know a little about dogs who says "I am sure your dog could win a prize in a show".

If your pet is purebred and his pedigree proves this to be so and he is registered at the Kennel Club then he can be shown. All pedigree dog shows in Britain are held under Kennel Club rules. You can write to the Club for information about the next show dates in your district. Alterna-

tively scan the small advertisements in the livestock section of your local paper, or buy one or two of the weekly dog newspapers or magazines to discover details of forth-coming dog shows.

One further requirement would be for your pet to pass a check by a vet on arrival at the show before gaining entry.

When you have picked a show that interests you telephone or write to the Show Secretary for details. There are various classifications according to the age, experience and sex of the animal you are going to exhibit. For example, a 'puppy' is shown between the ages of six and twelve months. No animal can be shown under the age of six months.

It is a good idea to visit a show or two first without your dog to see how things are run and to get a feeling of the atmosphere. You will see some shows held outdoors have marquees providing cover if the weather turns bad; other shows are held in large halls. Outdoor shows may be 'unbenched', indoor shows are as a rule 'benched', that is to say, individual pens are provided for each dog exhibited. The smaller breeds are sometimes penned on table high benches.

It is no use approaching a dog show thinking you will

69

tidy your pet up in the last day or two. Months in advance you should be concentrating on giving your pet the perfect combination of diet, exercise and grooming to bring him into the peak of condition. At the same time with reference to specific books on exhibiting the breed you should train your pet to walk on the lead and to stand and display himself properly for the judges. You should also make certain that he will get on well with other dogs in the show ring, since a dog which bites or fights will quickly be counted out. Keep your eye and attention firmly on the judge and do as he asks, and whether you win or lose it pays in the long run to accept the judgement graciously.

You do not have to have a pedigree dog to enter an 'exemption' dog show. Thousands take place all over the country all the year round. They are held under the exemption licence from the Kennel Club and people turn up on the day with their dogs to enter them in the show.

There are classes for pedigrees only and others confined to mongrels.

There are also classes where all dogs can compete against each other, e.g. on condition and obedience. There may be novelty classes to find the happiest dog or the one most resembling its owner.

Many dog owners prefer 'exemption' shows to the big championship events, where most of the exhibitors take everything so seriously that the sheer enjoyment of it all is lost.

Police Dogs—How They are Trained

A shining example to anyone who has ever wished to train a dog is provided by Britain's police dogs.

Millions of animal lovers marvel at the apparently reliable behaviour of these animals and the way they respond swiftly and accurately to their handler's commands.

With police dogs too, the whole secret of training is praise and reward for doing well and according to the Chief Instructor of Britain's biggest police dog training school at Keston in Kent, that means kind words and gentle hands.

At this particular school they not only train dogs with police officers to work in the Metropolitan force in London but also train dogs for police forces elsewhere in the country and in various parts of the world.

It is the gentle hands which are the most important aid in police dog training. "The hands are *never* used to hit the dog," says the chief instructor, "the dog associates them only with praise".

When a dog at any stage of his training, or after for that matter, has pleased his handler, he makes much fuss of the dog using hands and kind words. There are definitely no sweets or treats given as bribes to a police dog.

The Metropolitan Police breed more than half of the

dogs that they need but they are always on the look-out for likely canine recruits. They will accept good tempered dogs between the ages of nine and eighteen months, particularly Alsatians and Labradors with good noses.

Sometimes dogs are donated to police forces by the public but they have to pass an 'entrant's exam' first.

Police dogs don't need fancy pedigrees but they do need to be physically fit and display an even temperament and good intelligence.

The Alsatian, or German Shepherd Dog, is acknowledged to be the best all round police dog.

The police still prefer to use the original name of German Shepherd for these dogs although most of us would normally know them as Alsatians.

It is not the only working breed which is used by police forces. Dobermann Pinschers, Rottweilers and Weimaraners are also popular, but used in smaller numbers.

Labradors have particularly sensitive noses and are chosen to be trained for the highly specialised work of sniffing out explosives, drugs or even people buried in the rubble of collapsed buildings.

Labradors, of course, are natural retrievers and some experts believe that their sense of smell is more than 1000 times keener than a human nose. It is no wonder that our pet dogs object to being taken into a smoky room or run a mile if any kind of scent or perfume is sprayed near them.

The puppies the police breed themselves are trained right from the initial stages in the basic essentials of house cleanliness and walking on a lead.

The very young dog goes to live in the handler's home and grows up in the family atmosphere. Quite often another police dog the handler already works with lives there. The senior dog is probably nearing retirement.

The handler must be careful that the young dog does not train or associate out of doors too much with the veteran. A young dog tends to rely very quickly on an older dog. That would not do for a police dog which must learn to be self sufficient.

The dogs usually retire at the age of nine or ten years and become the pets of the handlers' families.

New dogs are given a week's official training at nine months old and it is at this age they can be best assessed for their suitability to continue any training to become a police dog.

A small percentage drop out. The reasons for failure can include being too soft, shy of traffic, too aggressive

THEIR KEEN SENSE OF SMELL IS INVALUABLE IN TRACKING MISSING PERSONS AND IN LOCATING SMUGGLED DRUGS

POLICE DOGS HAVE TO BE TRAINED TO IGNORE NOISE AND MOVEMENT AND CROWDS AND TO OBEY COMMANDS WITHOUT HESITATION

to other dogs and cats, or temperamentally unsuitable.

After training, police dogs can be used on all sorts of exciting assignments, from sniffing out drugs to catching bank robbers or guarding the Queen.

Police dog puppies officially meet their new handlers for the first time when they are 12 weeks old. At that age, They will have had the second of two vaccinations that will protect them against the 'killers'—canine distemper, hepatitis and leptospirosis.

At 12 weeks, the pup will be on four small meals a day of biscuit and milk, with meat in the evening. Vitamins and minerals are added to give them strong bones and teeth.

At 12 weeks there is a three day course of elementary training when the puppy learns to wear a collar, walk on his handler's left side and come to heel when called.

The dog's name needs to be short and sharp, one that he can easily recognise, learn and respond to.

Police puppies must learn to understand the world about them so they can adjust to, and cope with, any situation.

This is one reason why the puppies go to live with the police handler's family. There, they will meet cats, dogs, children, the noises and everyday things we take for granted.

They must get accustomed to traffic so they will be taken for walks in busy streets. At first their walks will be short and then gradually longer until they can sit and watch anything from motorbikes to big lorries without turning a hair.

There are regular monthly medical checks. Their weight and general progress is logged.

Alsatian puppies stay on four meals a day until around seven months old when they begin to lose interest in their milky supper. By this age they are quite used to meeting people and travelling about in a vehicle. They will have learnt to swim and 'speak on command'. The puppy learns to bark only when he is told to.

By this time, the puppy is also learning to retrieve, picking up objects and holding them for the handler. There is always plenty of praise and fuss made of the puppy but no titbits for a trainee police dog.

Police dogs are not kept indoors in carpeted centrally heated comfort but are housed in the handler's garden instead. They live in a standard green painted police kennel. This is because to be an effective working dog, they must grow the thick two-layered coat that is characteristic of the Alsatian.

IT NEEDS PRACTICE TO GET THEM TO SWIM LONGER DISTANCES AND IN RESPONSE TO AN ORDER

SPEAK, RINTY

DOGS TAKE TO WATER QUITE NATURALLY BUT USUALLY ONLY GO A A SHORT WAY BEFORE RETURNING TO THE BANK

THE POLICE TRAIN DOGS TO BARK ON COMMAND, FOR EXAMPLE WHEN FINDING A 'SUSPECT'

The coarse, waterproof top layer of long hair covers a dense soft coat which provides insulation. This natural combination keeps the dog warm and dry in the worst of weathers. The coat would not develop properly if the dog was housed indoors.

At nine or ten months, the young dog and handler return to the police dog training establishment for their one week initial training course when the dog's abilities are carefully assessed.

It is at this point that a dog which is not shaping up well is likely to fail. A dog which does not complete the course will usually be sold and become a family pet, a very well trained one at that. Reasons for failure can include shyness of traffic or noise, constant cat chasing or lacking the necessary physical or mental make-up to be a satisfactory police dog.

Over the next few months, the dogs learn to retrieve and carry out simple obedience and agility exercises.

When just over a year old, handler and dog take part in a 14 week intensive training course. At the end of this, the dog will be a fully operational working police dog.

It is hard packed 14 weeks, with many standards to attain, but all the lessons are made enjoyable for the dog.

The handlers must be careful on agility exercises not to make the jumps too high before the dogs' legs strengthen.

At the beginning of the course the jumps will not be much more than two feet high. If the dog was hurt by a heavy landing, he could be put off jumping for life. By the time they have finished, the dogs must be able to scale a six foot wall and make a long jump exceeding nine feet.

The dog must be taught to track. This means being able to follow a random trail of a 'suspect' and to find dropped articles. He must be able to track for at least

A POLICE DOG STARTS ON JUMPS NOT MUCH MORE THAN TWO FEET HIGH. IF A DOG WERE TO BE HURT BY A HEAVY LANDING HE COULD BE PUT OFF

AS HIS LEGS STRENGTHEN, HE IS PUT TO HIGHER AND LONGER JUMPS. EVENTUALLY HE WILL GO OVER A SIX FOOT WALL AND MAKE A LONG JUMP OF OVER NINE FEET

one hour by the end of training.

The dogs are taught to seek. This is like hide and seek, sometimes using an air scent to find people. When located, the dog must stand and bark to mark his man.

Dogs are required to chase, to run after a man, seize and hold him by the right arm. Training also continues in general obedience, in searching for lost property and developing the dog's ability to long-jump and scale walls.

Lessons are designed to be well within the dog's capabilities so that he succeeds every time. This way his confidence is built up.

Further training is given to bring out more character and determination in the dog. Lessons take place at night and under different weather conditions, since much of a police dog's effective work takes place then.

By the time the dog is 16 months old, he will be down to one substantial meal as a reward at the end of his day's work.

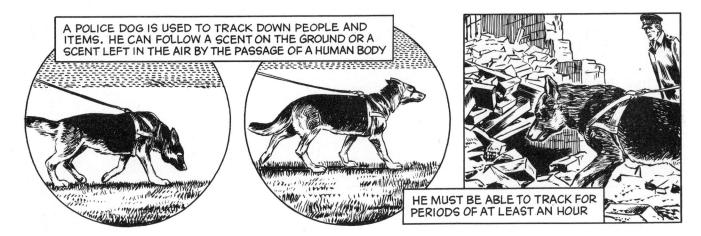

A POLICE DOG IS USED TO TRACK DOWN PEOPLE AND ITEMS. HE CAN FOLLOW A SCENT ON THE GROUND OR A SCENT LEFT IN THE AIR BY THE PASSAGE OF A HUMAN BODY

HE MUST BE ABLE TO TRACK FOR PERIODS OF AT LEAST AN HOUR

A successful dog will qualify at about 18 months and then go on patrol, but it will still build up experience every day.

Initially, the dogs' records will not show them as being fully experienced or 'hard'. They would not normally be called into a tough situation, say to face armed criminals. But at first, jobs such as searching for lost children are the normal routine. A dog's tracking ability plus a good nose enable it to be most effective at this work.

At the end of training, there is a passing out parade where handler and dog are awarded a certificate and the handler's family, who normally only see the dog as a 'pet' around the home, get the chance to see him really work out in a display.

When the dogs are about two years old, they return to the training centre for a refresher course designed to toughen them up. They will, for example, be asked to chase and arrest a suspect who carries a gun and fires blank shots at them.

There is a lot to be learnt from watching police dogs at work or going to see them in displays. Their basic training is virtually the same as any pet dog should receive. How they behave when trained to an advanced level just goes to show what patience and kindness can achieve with a dog.

Feeding Your Dog

A puppy starts to lap at about the age of three weeks. Until then, puppies rely on their mother's milk for all their nutritional requirements. Puppies grow quickly and from about three or four weeks are able to begin moving about and exploring their surroundings.

About now, they will begin to accept solid food but only in very small quantities, say a teaspoonful at a time. Puppies have small stomachs so they need to eat little and often. At this age, they develop quickly and become more active every day.

At six weeks old, puppies need four small meals a day. By the time they are three months, they can cope with three, larger meals each day; at eight months old, two meals a day are sufficient.

By the time a dog is one year old, only one meal a day is required. There are some exceptions among the very large breeds like Danes, Wolfhounds and, for that matter, Alsatians, which may benefit from more than one meal a day up to an age of around eighteen months. You should be guided by the breeder or someone who knows well the breed of dog you are keeping.

The first solid food a puppy eats should be palatable and easy to chew and swallow. In this respect there are a number of prepared proprietary canned and packeted

WHEN HE IS THREE MONTHS OLD, CUT HIM DOWN TO THREE MEALS EACH DAY. BY THE TIME HE IS A YEAR OLD, A SINGLE LARGE EVENING MEAL SHOULD BE SUFFICIENT FOR ALL EXCEPT THE BIGGEST BREEDS. HE CAN HAVE A FEW BISCUITS AND PERHAPS A DRINK OF WEAK TEA FOR BREAKFAST. NOTHING ELSE

A CLEAN BOWL OF FRESH WATER SHOULD ALWAYS BE AVAILABLE TO QUENCH HIS THIRST

A PUPPY HAS A SMALL STOMACH AND SHOULD HAVE FOUR MEALS A DAY. THE FOOD SHOULD BE IN SMALL, EASILY CHEWED PIECES

IT IS NATURAL FOR A DOG TO EAT QUICKLY, SO DON'T SCOLD HIM FOR BAD MANNERS

puppy foods which are ideal. Manufacturers spend a great deal of time, money and care on researching the best foods to make for puppies and adult dogs, so do not dismiss the products of the well known and reputable manufacturers.

Feeding canned foods to dogs is one way of being sure they are getting a balanced diet and it is a relatively economical method of feeding since there should be little or no waste.

Puppies and dogs, unlike cats, are not fastidious eaters and the appearance and regularity with which the same food is presented to them does not bother them in any way. If it likes the taste, and the food is the right size and easy for it to eat, a dog will be quite happy to scoff the same food day after day. As often as not, the owners ring the changes because they get bored with serving the same food and give the dog a variety for their own peace of mind.

HALF A DOG'S DIET SHOULD BE MEAT— LIGHTLY BOILED BEEF, HORSEFLESH, OFFAL, LIVER (NOT TOO FREQUENTLY). HARD LUMPS AND GRISTLE ARE GOOD FOR DIGESTION. MIX WITH DOG BISCUITS, STALE BROWN BREAD, GREENS, AND OTHER VEGETABLES

NEVER GIVE A DOG POTATOES, CAKES AND PASTRIES, SWEETS, AND BONES WHICH SPLINTER (SUCH AS CHICKEN, TURKEY, SHOULDER BLADES AND RIBS OF LAMB)

CANNED AND PACKAGED DOG FOODS ARE CONVENIENT AND RELATIVELY ECONOMICAL. A DOG WILL LIKE SOME BRANDS, DISLIKE OTHERS

On the other hand, it is a fact that a varied diet is a healthy diet, so there is no reason why you should not use canned and other proprietary foods as a matter of convenience and prepare your own doggy dishes when fresh foods are available.

Give your dog beef, horsemeat, liver (not too often), lights, paunches and offal—preferably very lightly boiled. Half your dog's diet should be meat, the rest dog biscuits, vegetables and greenstuffs. Do not give it potatoes since most dogs are unable to digest them. Milk can be given as a supplement but it should be treated as a food, not a drink.

Do not get into the habit of giving your puppy or dog sugar, sweets, cakes or pastry. Small bones are something else to avoid. Chicken or turkey bones are particularly dangerous since they are light, easy to crunch and break into dangerous splinters which can injure a dog by puncturing the throat or digestive tract.

Many flat bones, like shoulder blades or ribs (particularly of lamb) are also liable to splinter. Some dog experts consider that large raw marrow bones should be given to dogs to help keep their teeth in good condition, providing they are not left so that the dog can crunch them up and swallow pieces. Some vets would like to ban giving dogs bones altogether.

Remember, a supply of fresh water must be made available to your pet at all times.

Whether you prepare meals yourself or use commercial products, be sensible about the quantity of food your pet requires and remove anything not eaten before it becomes tainted. Many of the reputable pet food manufacturers now label their products with suggestions about the amount of food required by dogs of different breeds or sizes.

A chart compiled by one manufacturer is shown opposite. This has been compiled after many years' work at the company's animal studies centre.

As a general guide, allow a puppy 1 oz. of food per day for every pound of his weight. Small and medium size dogs are fully grown at nine months to a year old and from then on need about $\frac{1}{2}$ oz. of food for every pound of their body weight.

It is a remarkable fact that a survey has shown one third of Britain's pet dogs are overweight.

Fat dogs are vulnerable to ill health and early death if they are not slimmed down.

Usually it is the owner who is to blame for dogs that become fat and lazy. Many owners it seems do not take enough trouble to provide the correct amount of food a dog needs. They err by being over-generous. Lack of exercise and pampering make matters worse.

The problems of an overweight dog usually increase with age. Arthritis, heart disease and respiratory trouble are common.

At best a fat dog will suffer a painful old age, but fatness can also shorten the animal's lifespan by two or three years.

It is difficult for some owners to recognise obesity in their pets. As a rule it is the heavily built breeds that are inclined to become fat unnoticed. Included in this list would be Labradors, Beagles, Dachshunds and Pugs. Breeds like Setters, Salukis or Afghans are much less liable to become overweight.

Although different breeds of dog vary very much in size and shape, there is a general rule that will indicate that your pet is overweight. Run your hands along both

DAILY FEEDING GUIDE   (Meaty diet – cans per day: one can is 13¼ oz or 374 g)

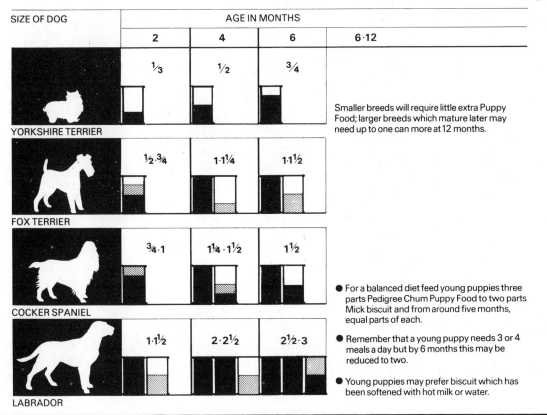

SIZE OF DOG	AGE IN MONTHS			
	2	**4**	**6**	**6·12**
YORKSHIRE TERRIER	⅓	½	¾	Smaller breeds will require little extra Puppy Food; larger breeds which mature later may need up to one can more at 12 months.
FOX TERRIER	½·¾	1·1¼	1·1½	
COCKER SPANIEL	¾·1	1¼·1½	1½	
LABRADOR	1·1½	2·2½	2½·3	

- For a balanced diet feed young puppies three parts Pedigree Chum Puppy Food to two parts Mick biscuit and from around five months, equal parts of each.

- Remember that a young puppy needs 3 or 4 meals a day but by 6 months this may be reduced to two.

- Young puppies may prefer biscuit which has been softened with hot milk or water.

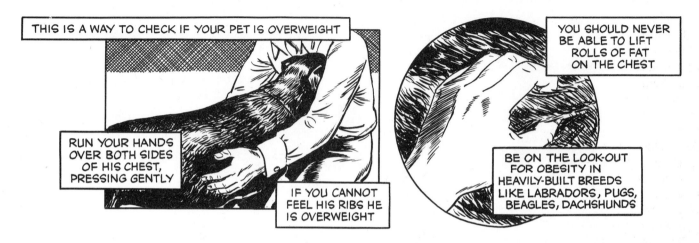

THIS IS A WAY TO CHECK IF YOUR PET IS OVERWEIGHT

RUN YOUR HANDS OVER BOTH SIDES OF HIS CHEST, PRESSING GENTLY

IF YOU CANNOT FEEL HIS RIBS HE IS OVERWEIGHT

YOU SHOULD NEVER BE ABLE TO LIFT ROLLS OF FAT ON THE CHEST

BE ON THE LOOK-OUT FOR OBESITY IN HEAVILY-BUILT BREEDS LIKE LABRADORS, PUGS, BEAGLES, DACHSHUNDS

sides of the animal's chest pressing gently with your fingertips. You should easily be able to feel the ribs of any dog, large or small, this way. If you can't feel the ribs, the dog is fat. You should NEVER be able to lift rolls of fat on the chest.

Although regular exercise is important it is the amount of food the dog eats that is most critical. A tiny quantity of extra food each day itself does not matter, but over a period of six months or so it will make a dog overweight.

If you think at any time that your dog should be put on a diet, it is wise to take your pet to the vet. The vet will advise you on a planned slimming campaign for your pet. Just as with humans, it is unwise to embark on a crash diet for a dog unless it is under medical supervision.

In fact, the problems of slimming for pets are virtually the same as for humans. The most easy approach is to cut down on carbohydrates, which means reducing the amount of biscuits or biscuit meal a dog eats. While doing this it is important to make sure that your pet is still eating enough vitamins and minerals. Lean meat alone is not good enough for dogs but most proprietary prepared foods including canned varieties contain balanced ingredients.

Do not expect results within a week. Any attempt to crash diet a dog will only make life miserable for you both. It may take three to six months with your pet's diet reduced by 50% to 70% of his original food intake, to show a marked improvement.

You must be careful to increase slightly the amount of food you give to your pet when the ideal weight is reached. If you do not do this, the weight loss will continue and you will be effectively starving your pet.

Remember, as with humans, when a dog is on a diet eating titbits, cakes and sweets between meals is taboo.

You and Your Dog

All dogs' lives are ruled by their natural instincts.

By appreciating what makes a dog act in the way it does you will be able to channel its natural behaviour into carrying out your instructions. You will also be able to steer your pet away from behaviour you do not wish to encourage. You will set yourself an impossible task, however, if you attempt to reverse what a dog does by instinct.

Over the years, desirable characteristics have been perpetuated by careful breeding, while undesirable characteristics have been toned down or bred out.

All dogs have the instinct to hunt. The instinct for hunting and running as a pack remains very strong in our domestic dogs. There are a number of types which have been bred for hunting purposes.

This behaviour is displayed in the tiniest pet dog when it chases squirrels or cats and becomes all the more bold at doing this if joined by some doggy companions. In some breeds of dog, the instinct to retrieve has been developed from the hunting instinct. Also the herding instinct can be traced to a hunting origin, the dog having been selectively bred to round up and head off animals but not to harm them.

Dogs lived in packs and that way they survived better.

DOGS SHARE MANY CHARACTERISTICS WITH THEIR WILD COUSINS

IN SOME BREEDS OF DOG IN PARTICULAR, AN INSTINCT TO RETRIEVE HAS BEEN DEVELOPED FROM THE HUNTING INSTINCT

POODLE POINTER

A PET DOG CHASING A SQUIRREL OR A CAT HAS THE SAME RUNNING AND HUNTING INSTINCT AS A WOLF

The ancestors of our pet dogs had a strong tendency to behave as pack animals. We can see this displayed by any pet dog wrongly allowed to roam in the street with other dogs. What may be a kind, tractable animal on his own, can become a demon when teamed up with one or more of his pals.

From the pack life stem the fighting and guarding instincts, since it was natural for a dog to protect not only himself but his territory and the rest of the pack which formed part of it. This instinct will cause a dog to fight. Males are more inclined to fight than bitches, although bitches sometimes fight and can become mortal enemies to each other.

The submissive instinct and the dog's instinct to fear are closely woven to produce the dog's mental constitution, in other words, they affect the temperament.

In some dogs there is quite a distinct homing instinct and there are a few, but nevertheless remarkable, tales of

DOGS ALLOWED TO ROAM THE STREETS FORM PACKS AND GET INVOLVED IN FIGHTS AND OTHER MISCHIEF. THEY REVERT IN MANY WAYS INTO A WILD STATE — CHASING, HUNTING AND SCAVENGING

WHAT CENTURIES OF DOMESTICATION HAS DONE IS TO DEVELOP DOGS' DESIRABLE CHARACTERISTICS AND TO TONE DOWN THE LESS DESIRABLE. EACH OWNER FACES SOMETHING OF THE SAME TASK WITH REGARD TO THE INDIVIDUAL DOG

dogs which have been lost and, guided by some sixth sense, have succeeded in finding their way home across country for distances of 100 miles or more.

The sex instinct has a significant effect on the behaviour of a dog or bitch. When the choice of buying a dog or bitch was considered we said dogs are more inclined to wander and bitches more inclined to stay at home. But for the most part, all bitches and dogs are easier to cope with as family pets if neutered. So consideration of the sex instinct is less significant. It can simply be removed if likely to pose a problem.

A most important instinct possessed by dogs is that of keeping their homes clean. Puppies will naturally try to avoid soiling their bedding material, basket or kennel.

Puppies purchased from kennels where they were kept in clean and tidy surroundings are likely to be much easier to house train properly than puppies bred under dirty conditions.

TRAIN THE DOG BY SHUTTING HIM IN A ROOM FOR A PERIOD WHEN YOU ARE HOME. SCOLD ANY WHIMPERS OF PROTEST THROUGH THE DOOR. AFTER HE HAS BEEN QUIET FOR SOME TIME, OPEN THE DOOR AND PRAISE HIM

A DOG THAT BARKS AND HOWLS WHENEVER HE IS LEFT ALONE UPSETS THE NEIGHBOURS

GOOD BOY, SAM

LATER ON, LEAVE THE HOUSE, GIVE THE DOG TEN MINUTES TO SETTLE DOWN, THEN RETURN AND SCOLD HIM IF HE IS BARKING. GO OUT AGAIN, OR THE DOG MAY GET THE IDEA THAT HE ONLY HAS TO MAKE A LOT OF NOISE FOR YOU TO RETURN AND STAY WITH HIM

A guard dog is only safe when it is accompanied by a handler it recognises and respects as its boss.

It is dangerous to give a dog which has known bad traits to a person who has no experience of it.

Large and powerful dogs which do not trust humans are potentially deadly weapons.

It is important when handling such a dog that a human being asserts himself as the 'pack leader'. Only then will the dog respect the handler.

A well adjusted dog that is trained to work with a man, and the man trained to work with that dog, makes for a reliable partnership. This is why police forces train one dog and one man to work together.

Dogs behave very much by instinct, and one that remains strong in a domestic animal is that of guarding whatever area it regards as its own territory.

A guard dog that only barks when his home ground is threatened by an intruder can be more effective than a dog that barks constantly.

Apart from the fact that persistent barking can be the cause of complaint by neighbours, it ceases to convey any real alarm. The fact that he goes on barking may turn out to be a handicap. His bark will cease to be regarded as an alarm by his owners.

An intruder may then be able to make friends with him, overcome or restrict him in some way or even feed him with dope. The only solution is for the dog to be properly trained as a guard.

Compulsive barking often as not is brought about by boredom. Sometimes it can be fear and on occasion a dog that barks consistently and hysterically may quite simply be a nutcase. If so, there is no cure.

Giving a dog that constantly barks a good hiding will only make it bark more.

Only by training, preferably in the company of his owner, is there a real chance of curing this bad habit in an adult dog.

Not all dogs are cut out to be good guards. The most efficient are those who have been trained from an early age.

Do not think if you go out and buy a big dog that is fully grown but without training you will end up with a

suitable guard. Such a dog is unlikely to have any real idea of what it is supposed to do, although its presence may prove a noisy deterrent.

Health and Hygiene
If your dog is to become an accepted member of the family the following rules should be followed:

Do not allow children to kiss pets, or dogs to lick children's faces. Dogs natually use their tongues to clean themselves and it is therefore unhygienic that they should then lick people.

Do not allow your dog to share your bed. Thousands do, though pets do not bath at night-time and they walk dirty streets all day without their paws covered.

Do not use the same feeding utensils or plates for dogs as for the rest of the family.

Feeding bowls should be washed up separately, and after those used by human members of the household.

Do not keep food sold solely for consumption by animals in close proximity to any food intended for human use.

SOME SENSIBLE RULES FOR HEALTH AND HYGIENE

DO NOT ALLOW CHILDREN TO KISS PETS, OR DOGS TO LICK CHILDREN'S FACES

DO NOT ALLOW THE DOG TO SHARE YOUR BED

DO NOT USE THE SAME FEEDING UTENSILS FOR DOGS AND FOR HUMANS

WASH THEIR FEEDING BOWLS SEPARATELY FROM YOUR DISHES

DO NOT KEEP DOG'S FOOD NEXT TO YOURS

DO NOT LET CHILDREN AND ANIMALS PLAY WITH THE SAME TOYS

Do not let children and animals play with the same toys.

Groom your dog regularly and thoroughly to make sure his coat is scrupulously clean and free from any kind of parasite like fleas.

Make sure that a puppy is thoroughly wormed under the guidance of a vet before it comes into the family, particularly if it is going to come into contact with young children.

If the puppy or dog mixes frequently with youngsters, it is a good idea to worm every six months as a safety precaution.

Everyone, particularly children, should be taught to wash their hands after handling a dog and before eating.

If these commonsense rules are followed as a matter of routine, they will neither seem tedious or complicated but will be sufficient to avoid even the remotest possibility of there being a health problem to your family created by your dog.

Remember, if your dog is off colour in any way, losing his coat, scratching or apparently distressed, consult your vet.

USE A SOFT BRISTLE BRUSH FOR A PUP BUT A STIFF BRISTLE BRUSH OR CURRY COMB LATER ON

BRUSH WITH THE GRAIN TO CLEAN OUT SURFACE HAIR, THEN AGAINST THE GRAIN TO CLEAN OUT THE UNDERCOAT, THEN WITH GRAIN TO RETURN HAIR TO ITS ORIGINAL POSITION. USE A COMB FOR EARS AND TAIL AND TO TEASE OUT TANGLES

TRIM NAILS WITH CLIPPER WHEN NECESSARY, MERELY REMOVING THE SHARP LITTLE HOOK AT THE TIP

Grooming

All dogs must be brushed vigorously for ten minutes every day. Long haired breeds will need more attention. Not only does this clean the coat, it also removes dead hair and tones up the skin and the circulation.

This routine should be followed at the same time each day. Use this as an opportunity to run your hands over your dog to examine him thoroughly each day for any bumps, lumps, and mats in his fur. At the same time, you should examine his coat closely for any burs, spiky grass seeds and unwanted parasites like fleas and ticks.

A regular check every day with hand and eye is the surest way of nipping any problem in the bud.

Talk to your pet in a reassuring tone of voice all the time you are doing this and he will become used to, and even look forward to, the invigorating grooming routine.

Check inside the dog's ears, between his toes and the pads of his feet for cuts, grass seeds or anything unusual.

PUT THE DOG IN FAIRLY DEEP TUB IN SEVERAL INCHES OF LUKEWARM WATER

USE A WASHRAG WITHOUT SOAP ON HEAD AND EARS, THEN USE DOG SOAP OR SHAMPOO TO LATHER THE REST OF HIM. THOROUGHLY RINSE OFF SOAP, THEN LIFT OUT IN BIG TOWEL

RUB HIM AS DRY AS POSSIBLE, AND KEEP HIM IN WARM UNTIL COMPLETELY DRY

You should start by grooming your dog's head and back. Then progress to the sides of the body, underneath and finish off with legs and tail.

A dog will seldom need bathing, if he is groomed thoroughly every day. Only bath a dog if he becomes very dirty or on the advice of your vet to remedy a skin or coat condition.

Bathing a dog is an event which requires a certain amount of planning and preparation. Choose a warm, dry day and bath the dog out of doors. Use a good quality shampoo or a mild soap that you might use yourself.

Ideally, you should run a shallow tin bath of water and place it outside on the ground. This time reverse the procedure you follow when grooming. Wash the animal's legs first, then its body and last of all its head. Then thoroughly rinse it down with plenty of luke warm, fresh water.

Remember, as soon as your pet 'escapes' from his tub he will stand and shake himself well, drenching anyone and everyone within range. Dry him thoroughly with his own rough towel.

Regular handling and grooming means that your pet becomes accustomed to being handled and this overcomes many of the problems likely to arise should you need to take your pet on an essential visit to the vet.

Travelling

If a dog is going to be a constant family companion, then sooner or later you will have to make a journey with him.

Possibly you will consider taking your dog on holiday with you as the better alternative to boarding him out in kennels you do not know.

Sooner or later then, your dog will have to become an acceptable traveller. It is a fact that many dogs suffer from travel sickness, especially car sickness, particularly when they are puppies. There are no hard and fast rules about the problem but the majority of dogs do grow out of it rather in the same way many children do.

If possible, it is a good idea to get a dog used to travelling in a car by taking him on short journeys to start with and by gradually extending these trips.

If the early journeys terminate with an enjoyable experience like a run in the park then the dog will associate the idea of travelling in the car with pleasure and even look forward to going out in the vehicle.

To reduce the likelihood of the dog being sick do not feed it for at least three or four hours before the journey. Also withdraw water some time before the dog goes out.

Good ventilation in the vehicle and fairly frequent stops will help the dog to acclimatise to travelling.

It is believed by some that if a dog is allowed to look out of the side windows of a car, the constant movement of traffic in the other direction can induce sickness. So if the dog is going to look out at all, it is considered better to allow the dog to look forward through the windscreen.

This means the dog becomes a front seat passenger which is all very well so long as other members of the family do not object and he is safely secured so that he cannot possibly interfere with the driver. Everyone must have seen at some time dogs sitting on drivers' laps; it may look funny but drivers who allow this are stupid and dangerous.

Ideally, the best place for a dog in a car is either on the floor or in estate-type cars confined behind a grille behind the rear seats. The dog needs only sufficient room to make itself comfortable but not enough room for it to become

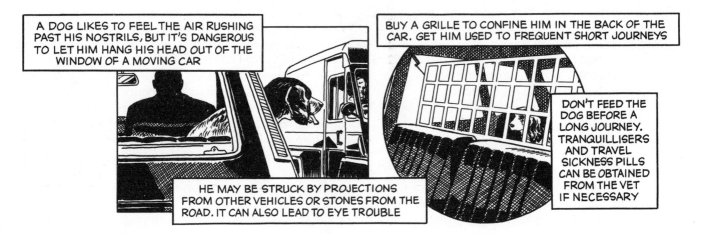

A DOG LIKES TO FEEL THE AIR RUSHING PAST HIS NOSTRILS, BUT IT'S DANGEROUS TO LET HIM HANG HIS HEAD OUT OF THE WINDOW OF A MOVING CAR

BUY A GRILLE TO CONFINE HIM IN THE BACK OF THE CAR. GET HIM USED TO FREQUENT SHORT JOURNEYS

DON'T FEED THE DOG BEFORE A LONG JOURNEY. TRANQUILLISERS AND TRAVEL SICKNESS PILLS CAN BE OBTAINED FROM THE VET IF NECESSARY

HE MAY BE STRUCK BY PROJECTIONS FROM OTHER VEHICLES OR STONES FROM THE ROAD. IT CAN ALSO LEAD TO EYE TROUBLE

bumped or thrown about.

It is also madness to allow a dog to put its head out of a car window when travelling. Apart from the risk of falling out or causing some sort of accident, the dog's eyes are likely to become painful as the result of exposure to wind and grit. Watery eyes, conjunctivitis and expense at the vet will be the result.

A small point but one worth remembering is that if there are any exhaust leaks, fumes are most likely to accumulate on the floor of the vehicle or to the rear. Any pets, dogs or cats in baskets or smaller pets in little boxes, which are placed on the floor in a car with a leaky exhaust are bound to suffer.

A final point to help the dog that is a perpetual bad traveller—tranquillising pills are available but only on the prescription of a veterinary surgeon. Their dosage needs careful calculation by him. They can be used to help a dog during essential journeys. You should consult your

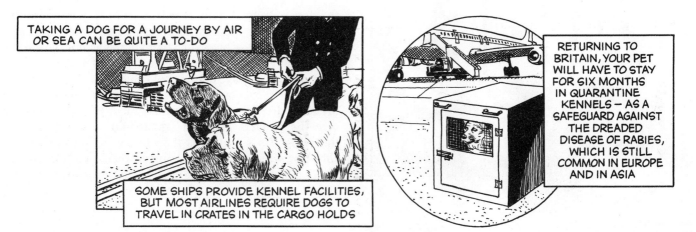

TAKING A DOG FOR A JOURNEY BY AIR OR SEA CAN BE QUITE A TO-DO

SOME SHIPS PROVIDE KENNEL FACILITIES, BUT MOST AIRLINES REQUIRE DOGS TO TRAVEL IN CRATES IN THE CARGO HOLDS

RETURNING TO BRITAIN, YOUR PET WILL HAVE TO STAY FOR SIX MONTHS IN QUARANTINE KENNELS — AS A SAFEGUARD AGAINST THE DREADED DISEASE OF RABIES, WHICH IS STILL COMMON IN EUROPE AND IN ASIA

veterinary surgeon about such drugs well in advance of the intended trip. Because of the strength of these drugs, some are scheduled poisons, they are sometimes not recommended in older animals or animals with a health problem.

The modern tranquillisers only obtainable from the vet have now really replaced the sedatives which used to be popular but which unfortunately had a number of alarming side effects.

Given some sedatives, it would become apparent to the owner that the dog needed to relieve itself every five minutes. At the end of a journey, sometimes a dog would be so sedated that it would be almost falling asleep on its feet. No joke in the case of a big dog. Just imagine trying to carry a seven stone dog-tired Alsatian!

If you are going to travel by air or by sea, check with your tour operator. Some ships may provide kennel facilities, but most airlines require that dogs travel in crates in the cargo holds. Also remember, that if you are bringing

The British Isles are free of rabies and wish to remain so. No animal may be landed there without having an import licence and undergoing quarantine, even if it has been vaccinated. If you are visiting Britain, it is recommended that you do not take your animals with you. (If you come in your own boat, the pet would have to be strictly confined on board throughout your visit.) To prevent the introduction of this fatal and expensive disease, severe penalties (heavy fines and up to a year's imprisonment) are imposed on anyone attempting to smuggle animals. Any illegally imported animal is liable to be destroyed.

DON'T SPOIL YOUR VISIT- KNOW THE REGULATIONS

Prepared for Her Majesty's Government by the Central Office of Information, 1976
Printed in England for Her Majesty's Stationery Office by Willsons Printers (Leicester) Ltd. Dd. 085037 Pro. 7666

ONE OF MANY GOVERNMENT POSTERS, PART OF A RABIES-AWARENESS CAMPAIGN

the dog back to Britain, it will have to stay in quarantine kennels for six months after you come back. Trying to smuggle your dog back into the country is not only stupid —it is dangerous. No matter how careful you have been, your dog could have contracted rabies, which is now widespread in Europe and Asia. Britain is, so far, free of this dreadful disease, mainly because most pet owners recognize the dangers involved and would rather be without their dogs for six months than lose them altogether. The silly few who attempt to smuggle their pets into Britain are liable to extremely heavy fines and inprisonment. And rightly so.

Calling the Vet

If your dog has an accident or develops any unusual symptoms, you should as soon as possible take your pet to the vet or call him in if necessary. Do not waste time with odd lotions and potions you think may do the trick.

Some fatal conditions can begin with the mildest of symptoms and the chances of your pet's recovery may become slimmer if you delay calling the vet.

If you feed and groom your dog regularly, you should

be the first person to notice if there is anything wrong.

The first sign that something may be amiss is if your dog's appetite fades, but note also the condition of his coat, his eyes, nose and mouth.

Some dogs may become irritable and not want to be touched, for example, if they have a bad tooth. Another sign of illness is the dog wanting to get away from people and spend a lot of time sleeping.

You should make a permanent note of your vet's telephone number and any other numbers necessary to contact him in an emergency out of normal surgery hours.

It is better if you get to know your vet before you need his help at short notice. If you visited him when you first acquired your puppy for a check-up and at the time of your pet's immunisations then you will be less likely to have any problems obtaining veterinary help in an emergency.

Except in genuine emergency, it is better to make an appointment to see a vet. These days, many of them who hold surgeries for small animals, like cats and dogs, are so busy that they only work on an appointment system.

In the same way that you might call your doctor, you should arrange to call the vet as early in the day as possible or, better still, the day before, to enable him to plan his case list.

You will be making your private vet's bill more expensive if you insist on calling him to you instead of taking your pet to the surgery.

Most vets would prefer you to go to the surgery anyway. They cannot get on with the work of curing sick animals so effectively if they are forever driving about the countryside or trying to find places to park.

Most vets will say they prefer to treat animals in the well equipped environment of their surgery. There, they have skilled assistants to hand to help manage the animals. At home on their own ground, dogs of all sizes will frequently misbehave and make the vet's job more difficult and treatment less efficient.

The animal welfare societies exist to treat sick animals belonging to people who are unable to afford the fees of private veterinary surgeons.

They do not make a normal practice of visiting patients, so the animal must be taken to the societies' clinics.

As a rule, they do not carry out work which is not directly treating sick animals. For example, tail-docking or any 'cosmetic' operations do not come within their activities and they do not give inoculations or spray bitches.

Should you need a vet at any time and do not have a

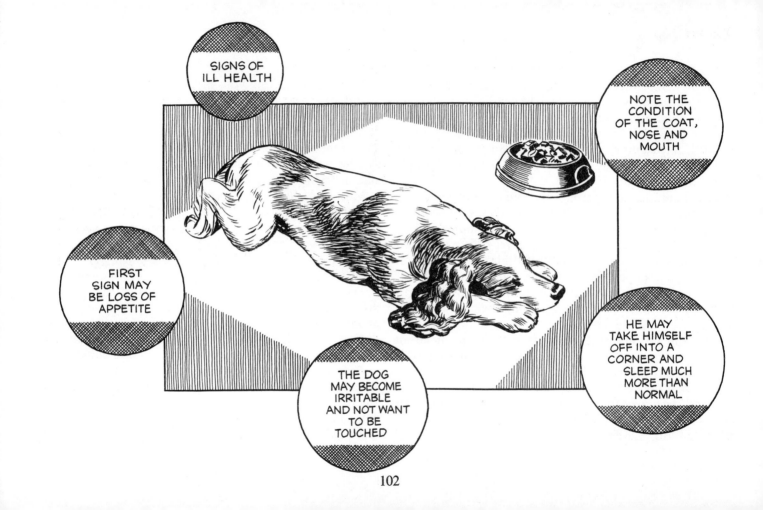

102

name or telephone number to hand, perhaps you are away on holiday, you can obtain the names of local vets in an emergency from the local police. The Automobile Association and the Royal Automobile Club also have lists of local vets.

The 'Yellow Pages' classified telephone directory, available in any post office, also lists the vets in the area under the heading 'Veterinary Surgeons and Veterinary Practitioners'. Also 'Animal Welfare Societies' are listed.

Keeping out of Trouble

If you allow other people to take your dog for a walk it can lead to trouble; this is especially true of children who offer to take the dog for a walk during school holidays.

Although a dog on his own may not cause trouble, pal him up with three or four other dogs, and you have a pack that may behave like a mob of hooligans. Groups of dogs can easily terrorise cyclists, children in playgrounds and quiet residential neighbourhoods. Let your pet out with

people you do not fully know and your pet may soon be in this band of trouble-makers.

Although a busy pet owner may be tempted to let neighbours' children take the dog for a walk, the wise owner will first go with them to see how they get on with the animal.

Few people seem to realise the risks involved in entrusting dogs to youngsters who cannot cope with them.

Owners can be held legally responsible for their dogs' misdeeds. The 1973 Animal Act spells out the owner's liability for accidents.

All dog owners should ask themselves, "If something goes wrong, what could be the consequences for me?"

Many general household insurance policies give third party protection to the householder in the event of damage or injury caused to others by his dog. Such a policy would not cover a child who was not a member of the same household.

You should check that as a dog owner you have third party insurance protection. If you have not, consult an insurance broker.

Worrying Farm Livestock
All dogs, large or small, have the instinct born in them to hunt. So a dog of any size is a potential sheep worrier.

It is part of a dog's behaviour pattern to chase and kill.

When they are in the countryside, all dog owners should remember the need to keep their pets on a lead whenever there are farm animals about.

A well aimed kick or butt from a cow or sheep can easily hurt the unwary dog, so keeping it on a lead is as much for its protection as for the farm animals'.

Once in the countryside, dogs can easily forget their

105

THOUGH MOST DOGS SLEEP INDOORS NOWADAYS, IT IS HEALTHY TO HAVE A KENNEL OUTSIDE IF THERE IS A FAIR-SIZED GARDEN

A RUNNING CHAIN IS SIMPLE TO ERECT AND CAN BE USED WHEN YOU WISH TO LEAVE THE DOG, FOR EXAMPLE WHILE SHOPPING

good town manners and do things you may not expect, such as chasing sheep.

Each year, on average, around 10,000 farm animals are killed or injured as a result of being chased by dogs.

Remember also that the owner or person in charge of a dog who allows it to worry livestock, can be fined for the first offence (£20) and much more heavily for a second or subsequent offence by the same dog (£50).

A court can order the dog to be destroyed and if a dog kills or injures livestock, the owner of the dog may be liable for the damage.

A farmer may successfully defend a civil action for killing or injuring any dog he finds worrying, or even about to worry, his farm animals.

The farmer will have to show that there was no other reasonable way of stopping the attack and he will have to inform the police within 48 hours of shooting the dog.

A great deal of damage is done in the early spring by

dogs chasing ewes that are pregnant. The distress to the ewe causes the lambs to be born prematurely and they die. But livestock-worrying by dogs is not just confined to the early spring, it is an all-the-year-round problem and you must make sure your dog never becomes part of it.

Running Chains
Although it is cruel to chain up a dog in a confined space, it is sometimes necessary to restrict your dog's range of activity for a limited time while you cannot directly keep an eye on him.

Running chains are a useful and practical solution. They allow the dog a considerable range of movement but, at the same time, prevent him from escaping or causing damage in parts of the garden where you do not want him to go.

It is quite simple to make a running chain between two anchor points, two posts, trees or rings in a wall. Tie a taut rope or wire between both points with a ring that runs freely along the length of it. Attach a length of light chain or a stout lead to this ring and clip the other end to the dog's collar.

Arrange a 'stop' on the line beyond which the travelling ring cannot pass. This prevents the dog becoming wound round a post or tree providing the anchorage.

Make sure the line is high enough to be out of the dog's way and that the chain the dog is attached to is long enough to allow it to lie down, enter its kennel or reach its food and water.

Dangers to Dogs
The following notes refer to less obvious hazards which from time to time we hear have serious consequences for dogs. Forewarned is forearmed. If any of the following is obvious—good, remember to someone it was not!

Never allow your pet to catch or play with a small ball, it may choke on it. Beware also of small toys or bones or anything likely to break into fragments. Chicken bones are notorious for this. The animal may be choked and swallowing foreign bodies can cause perforation or obstruction of the gut. Elastic bands, buttons, etc., can all be dangerous.

Never place elastic bands around neck or limb, if forgotten they cut in and cause serious injury.

DOGS LIKE EXPLORING ODD CORNERS, SO TAKE CARE TO COVER SHARP EDGES AND TINS OF POISONOUS SUBSTANCES

A SMALL CUT CAN BE CLEANED BY A DISINFECTANT SOLUTION, A CUT ON THE PAW CAN BE DIPPED INTO A BOWL OF THE SOLUTION

A 'LAMP SHADE' COLLAR OF CARDBOARD PREVENTS A DOG LICKING A WOUND

Never allow your pet on to thin ice.

Never walk your dog, even on a lead, so it is between you and the traffic; at the least it may be struck and cut by stones or in winter by ice thrown from passing vehicles.

Never allow your dog off the lead anywhere near garden or agricultural chemicals, farm animals, the railway, quarries or cliff tops.

Do not allow your dog to swim in deep water, flowing rivers or the sea.

Never allow your pet to drink from puddles, ditches or ponds which may be polluted.

Sex and the Single Dog

Is it unfair to deny a pet dog or bitch the opportunity to breed? The answer, generally, is no. Dogs often make better and more contented companions if they are not used for breeding.

It is not advisable for the health and happiness of a male dog to give him the opportunity to mate. To do so would only arouse instincts which would make him unsuitable as a household pet. He may become a nuisance to himself and develop bad habits which are a nuisance to his owners.

The majority of pet dogs settle down contentedly if they are not used for breeding. It is far better that breeding should be left to stud dogs kept by kennels.

In Britain, vets generally do not castrate male dogs unless there is a definite reason. It is far more usual to neuter bitches.

Some people believe it is unfair to deny bitches the opportunity to produce a litter of puppies but it is a fallacy that having one litter of puppies does a bitch good. All that happens is that her mothering instincts are aroused and then you deny her the opportunity of having another family. Additionally, you have the responsibility of finding good homes for the puppies. Sometimes, particularly when the puppies are mongrels, that is not easy.

Today more and more owners of bitches are having their

pets operated on to prevent them from breeding as a matter of course and, for example, all the bitches which are trained by the Guide Dogs for the Blind Association are spayed before they go out to work. This is essential as the guide dogs' work is continuous and they must at no time be distracted by other dogs.

In fact it is a good idea to have a bitch neutered as she is more likely to settle down and be a contented pet. Neutering is the only *permanent* way to avoid unwanted families of puppies. It also avoids the nuisance created by her trying to get out when in season or by dogs in the neighbourhood being attracted to her. The trouble is, as we have said, this is an expensive operation and can cost between £20 and £30.

Some owners object to having bitches spayed on the grounds that they may get fat. But in fact the weight and shape of a dog or bitch depends largely on diet and the amount of exercise given. The right food and sufficient exercise will normally prevent any dog from becoming too fat.

Should a bitch be accidentally mated when in season, or if she succeeded in her efforts to slip out and you are not certain what happened while she was out of your sight, you can prevent an unwanted pregnancy by contacting the vet quickly.

Get her to a local private veterinary surgeon as soon as possible, preferably within 24 hours, and he will be able to give her a single intra-muscular hormone injection which should prevent unwanted puppies.

Be warned, your pet will come into season again from that time and so could produce puppies if mated again a week or two after the injection.

Although the injection may cost several pounds, it will work out much cheaper than having unwanted puppies to rear and the problem of finding them good homes.

If you do not want your pet spayed, then pills are available on the prescription of private vets to postpone her season temporarily.

This method of birth control would work out quite expensive if used over a long term but some owners of bitches find it very convenient since it enables them to take their bitches to pre-arranged dates like shows or holidays without the inconvenience at that time which would have been caused by them being in season.

Various proprietary preparations are available which are designed to be sprinkled on the coat of a bitch when in season to hide the odour which attracts dogs.

These preparations sometimes only have a limited effect

IF YOU WANT TO MATE YOUR PET, CONTACT ESTABLISHED BREEDERS THROUGH THE KENNEL CLUB

ROUGH-HAIRED DACHSHUND

THE SIMPLEST ARRANGEMENT IS FOR A STUD FEE TO BE PAID TO THE OWNER OF THE DOG, WITH AN UNDERTAKING THAT IF THE BITCH DOES NOT CONCEIVE SHE IS MATED A SECOND TIME FREE OF CHARGE

PROFESSIONAL BREEDERS OFTEN SET DOWN THEIR 'BREEDING TERMS' IN WRITING AND LODGE A THIRD COPY WITH THE KENNEL CLUB

THINK VERY SERIOUSLY HOWEVER BEFORE TRYING TO TURN A FAMILY PET INTO A STUD DOG OR A BREEDING BITCH

in disguising her condition and deterring dogs, but they certainly do not prevent breeding.

When people who are not experienced dog breeders decide to arrange a 'marriage' for their pets, they can, instead, be starting a dog fight where even the best of friends fall out.

Professional breeders often set down their 'breeding terms' in writing and lodge a third copy with the Kennel Club. It prevents all the snapping and snarling that can go on between two owners if they breed what they believe to be a valuable litter and have not already decided between themselves how the puppies should eventually be shared.

Even if they have given this problem some thought, Nature can sometimes throw a spanner in the works by producing only one puppy.

The simplest arrangement is for a stud fee to be paid to the owner of the dog, with an undertaking that if the bitch does not conceive, she is mated a second time free of charge.

If you want to become involved in dog breeding, then the best way to do so is to contact established breeders through the Kennel Club.

Talk to your vet and read books on the subject; there are usually plenty to be found in local libraries.

You should think seriously before trying to turn an ideal family pet into a stud dog or a breeding bitch.

First Aid

Some dogs, like some people, never have a day's illness in their lives. But it is as well to know how to cope if your pet is sick or has an accident.

If you are nursing a sick dog at home, keep the patient as quiet as possible and in darkened surroundings.

Warmth should be provided, by using a hot water bottle. Metal or stone bottles are best for pets. Do not fill the bottle with boiling water, but use hot water. Wrap the hot water bottle in a blanket and place it next to the patient to provide a steady source of warmth.

Follow any instructions that your vet gives you to the letter. It is not a bad idea to number and write on a post-card the instructions your vet gives you so that you follow the routine he has prescribed exactly and nothing is forgotten.

When a dog is suffering from any kind of irritation and is constantly attempting to bite or scratch itself, a 'lampshade' collar placed around the neck to partly enclose the head is valuable. It will prevent a dog from constantly biting and worrying at a bandaged paw or, alternatively, stop him from scratching continuously at an ear that may be irritating him.

An important point to remember about nursing any sick animal at home is that you do not relax your attention too

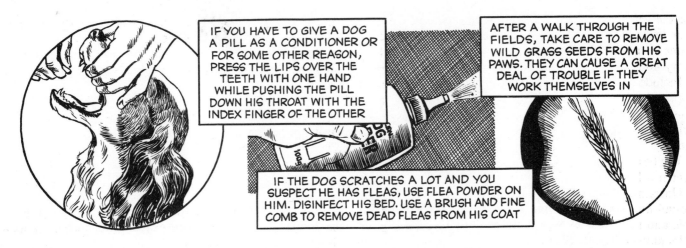

IF YOU HAVE TO GIVE A DOG A PILL AS A CONDITIONER OR FOR SOME OTHER REASON, PRESS THE LIPS OVER THE TEETH WITH ONE HAND WHILE PUSHING THE PILL DOWN HIS THROAT WITH THE INDEX FINGER OF THE OTHER

AFTER A WALK THROUGH THE FIELDS, TAKE CARE TO REMOVE WILD GRASS SEEDS FROM HIS PAWS. THEY CAN CAUSE A GREAT DEAL OF TROUBLE IF THEY WORK THEMSELVES IN

IF THE DOG SCRATCHES A LOT AND YOU SUSPECT HE HAS FLEAS, USE FLEA POWDER ON HIM. DISINFECT HIS BED. USE A BRUSH AND FINE COMB TO REMOVE DEAD FLEAS FROM HIS COAT

soon.

The effects of some diseases, like distemper, can last eight weeks or more. Distemper will make a dog obviously ill for a period of three weeks or so, but it may be two months or more before the debilitating effects are gone so the patient still needs care.

Prevention is, of course, better than a cure and the best insurance you can take out to maintain your pet's health is to see that he is inoculated against the common illnesses and make sure his jabs are kept up-to-date.

Good food, plenty of exercise and clean, warm, dry accommodation are fundamental requirements.

Your dog may be your best friend, but if he is ill, your dog's best friend must always be the vet.

You must never attempt to treat your dog if its condition is any more than plainly trivial. You should call the vet for advice. First aid should be confined only to making the animal safe and reasonably comfortable while waiting

First Aid

for the vet.

A first aid kit for your dog can be made up to keep at home or take on holiday to deal with simple mishaps. Pack everything in a tin to keep the contents clean and dry.

Include several bandages of different widths. When you apply a bandage, never tie it tightly or secure it with safety pins. Safety pins are easily opened by a dog's mouth and will cause an even bigger problem if your pet swallows them!

The best way to secure a bandage or dressing is to apply over it a length of medicated sticky plaster.

Untrained people may apply a temporary dressing on a wound by applying a wad of lint or linen over the affected area and then binding it gently over with adhesive tape.

Include a pair of sharp scissors to cut bandage and adhesive tape, or trim fur if necessary. Choose a pair with round blunt ends and so avoid the risk of puncturing the dog's skin.

A small bottle of non-poisonous antiseptic for application to scratches or grazes is a useful addition. This should be diluted if necessary and applied according to the manufacturers' instructions.

Do not put old medicines of any kind in the first aid kit unless your vet has told you that they will keep. Some medicines when they are stored change with age and may have the wrong effect or none at all.

Do not give human medicines to dogs unless your vet suggests something to you on the 'phone that you may use as a temporary measure.

Broken Bones

The dog must be kept as still and quiet as possible until the vet's help has been obtained. Most dogs can be carried on the back seat of a car, wrapped up carefully in a blanket or old coat.

Small dogs should be settled comfortably in a ventilated box or in the bottom of a basket with a secure lid from which they cannot escape. Disposable cardboard pet containers used in an emergency are cheap and hygienic. They can be obtained from pet stores and some animal welfare clinics.

Burns and Scalds

In the event of an electrical burn *turn off the power* and pull out the plug before doing anything at all.

The area burnt should be washed quickly and continuously with quantities of cold water. This is to dissipate

115

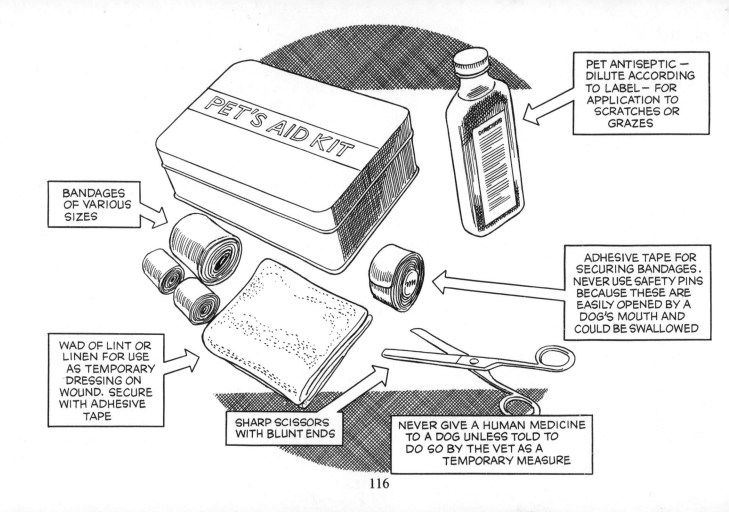

PET ANTISEPTIC —
DILUTE ACCORDING
TO LABEL — FOR
APPLICATION TO
SCRATCHES OR
GRAZES

BANDAGES
OF VARIOUS
SIZES

ADHESIVE TAPE FOR
SECURING BANDAGES.
NEVER USE SAFETY PINS
BECAUSE THESE ARE
EASILY OPENED BY A
DOG'S MOUTH AND
COULD BE SWALLOWED

WAD OF LINT OR
LINEN FOR USE
AS TEMPORARY
DRESSING ON
WOUND. SECURE
WITH ADHESIVE
TAPE

SHARP SCISSORS
WITH BLUNT ENDS

NEVER GIVE A HUMAN MEDICINE
TO A DOG UNLESS TOLD TO
DO SO BY THE VET AS A
TEMPORARY MEASURE

the heat. If the vet cannot attend immediately, the area of the burn can meanwhile be bathed with a solution made by adding a heaped teaspoonful of bicarbonate of soda to a pint of tepid water.

Choking

Puppies in particular are especially susceptible to swallowing small objects—buttons, toy soldiers, hairgrips—in fact anything goes. The danger is that so many of these items are now made from plastic-like materials that they cannot be detected by the vet's X-ray equipment.

Prevention is better than cure and you should always be on the look-out for any small object of the animal's attention. If you spot your puppy quietly chewing away, take whatever it is out of his mouth and give him a 'tasty hide' chew to work on.

Avoid giving dogs small bones, balls or toys. Should a foreign body become lodged in the animal's mouth between its teeth or in its throat, this is a job for the vet. Dogs which go off their food sometimes have small sharp objects like pins, needles or grass seed barbs lodged in their throats. Puppies frequently swallow needles after playing with a thread, and tiny fishbones can lodge in their throats. This will prevent them from eating and often a great deal of skill is required by the vet to remove them.

Cuts, Bites and Grazes

The wound should be thoroughly cleansed. In all aspects of first aid, hygiene is very important, As a temporary measure, the best way to stop bleeding is to press over the injury a dry pad of lint which is firmly secured with bandage and tape until the vet can be consulted.

Ears

Bites and cuts on the flap of the ear often bleed freely. The result is often dramatic and looks much worse than it is. If the dog shakes its head, although the injuries involved may be quite insignificant, blood tends to be splashed everywhere.

During late summer and autumn it is not unusual for dogs with long ears to get grass seeds in the ear. The wicked dart-like heads of wild barley are notorious for this. They can cause the animal considerable distress. The owner should make no attempt to extract anything from the inside of the ear. This job is best left to the vet.

Eyes

If you must remove debris from your pet's eyes, you should use quantities of clean water as an emergency measure. Given a little more time you should make up a saline solution using one teaspoon of salt thoroughly dissolved in one pint of luke warm water. Eyes are very delicate and professional help should be sought whenever needed.

Fits

Puppies are particularly prone to convulsions when they are teething. Although a puppy in a convulsed state is most distressing to watch, usually there are no serious consequences. No attempt should be made to touch the animal until the fit is over when it should be placed in a darkened room and kept as quiet as possible from disturbance by other people and pets. Consult your vet.

Poisoning

This can only be dealt with by the vet. He should be seen without delay. In some areas, notably on dry moors, heaths and hillsides, inquisitive dogs are sometimes bitten on the nose or paws by vipers. Local vets frequently have a supply of anti-snake-bite serum.

If you are away from home you must act immediately. If you do not know a vet nearby, you should telephone the police for assistance.

Poisoning by swallowing something is usually demonstrated by the dog foaming at the mouth or salivating, breathing rapidly and perhaps heavily, a rapidly accelerated heartbeat and staggering about drunkenly. Get someone to make a rapid search for the cause of the poisoning while you are on the way to the vet with your pet.

Stings

A dog, even a large one, can be killed by wasp or bee stings. If stung on the tongue or inside the mouth, the resultant swelling has been known to choke dogs to death. When a dog is stung, if the sting can be seen it should be quickly removed and the region pinched to localise the spread of the poison.

Some immediate relief can be given in the case of a wasp sting by applying vinegar to the inflamed area and in the case of a bee sting, by applying a paste of moistened salt to the swelling.

Glossary of Dog Terms

Apple headed
Dogs with domed heads like Chihuahuas or Griffons.

Bitch
Female dog.

B.I.S.
Best in Show.

Brindle
A coat colour created by a mixture of light and dark streaks of grey or brown, e.g. many greyhounds.

Brush
A bushy tail.

Champion
In Britain, a dog or bitch that has won three Challenge Certificates at championship shows under different judges.

Cropping
The practice of cutting the ears of certain breeds, e.g. Boxers and Dobermanns. Occurs on continent, frowned on in Britain.

Cryptorchid
A dog without descended testicles. Cannot be exhibited.

Dew-claw
Small vestigial claws found on the inside foot clear of the ground. Usually removed since can cause problems by ingrowing.

Distemper
A highly infectious virus disease that mainly affects young dogs.

Docking
Practice of removing puppies' tails leaving recognised lengths, e.g. many pedigree breeds.

Entropion
Painful condition caused by inward growing eyelashes.

Hip Dysplasia
Several abnormal conditions of the joint of the femur with the hip often causing lameness of the back legs.

Hock
The dog's 'ankle' joint below the stifle joint.

Merle
A coat colour of bluish grey with black streaks, e.g. seen in some Collies and Shetland Sheepdogs.

Over-shot
Upper teeth project in front of lower teeth.

P.R.A.
Progressive Retinal Atrophy. Hereditary loss of sight in some breeds.

Roan
A coat colour caused by a mixture of coloured hairs with white, e.g. many Spaniels.

Stifle-joint
Dog's 'knee' joint.

Stop
The depression in a dog's face above the nose.

Undercoat
Soft furry layer under the longer outer hair that gives added weather protection to breeds such as Alsatians.

Undershot
Teeth in lower jaw project in front of top set of teeth.

Wall eyed
Eyes showing white or blue in iris, sometimes seen in Collies.

Animal Welfare Societies and Useful Addresses

Animal Health Trust,
  24, Portland Place, London, W1N 4HN.
Animal Welfare Trust,
  47, Whitehall, London, SW1A 2BZ.
Blue Cross,
  1, Hugh Street, Victoria, London, SW1V 1QQ.
British Horse Society,
  National Equestrian Centre, Stoneleigh, Kenilworth, Warwickshire, CV8 2LR.
British Union for the Abolition of Vivisection,
  (Pet Home-finding Service),
  47, Whitehall, London, SW1A 2BZ.

British Veterinary Association,
  7, Mansfield Street, London, W1M 0AT.
Cage & Aviary Birds,
  Surrey House, 1, Throwley Way, Sutton, Surrey, SM1 4QQ.
Cats Protection League,
  29, Church Street, Slough, Berkshire, SL1 1PW.
Glasgow and West of Scotland Society for the Prevention of Cruelty to Animals,
  15, Royal Terrace, Glasgow G3 7NY, Scotland.
Governing Council of the Cat Fancy,
  The Secretary, Dovefields, Petworth Road, Witley,

Surrey, GU8 5QW.
Guide Dogs for the Blind Association,
Alexandra House, 113, Uxbridge Road, Ealing, **London**, W5 5TQ.
International League for the Protection of Horses,
P.O. Box No. 166, 67A, Camden High Street, **London**, NW1 7JL.
International Society for the Protection of Animals,
106, Jermyn Street, London, SW1Y 6EE.
Irish Society for the Prevention of Cruelty to **Animals**,
1, Grand Canal Quay, Dublin 2, Ireland.
The Jerry Green Foundation Trust,
The Jay Gee Animal Sanctuary, Broughton, **Brigg**, South Humberside, DN20 0BJ.
Kennel Club of Great Britain,
1, Clarges Street, Piccadilly, London, W1Y 8AB.
League against Cruel Sports Limited,
1, Reform Row, London, N17 9TW.
Ministry of Agriculture, Fisheries and Food,
(Animal Exports and Imports),
Animal Health Division, Government Buildings, Hook Rise South, Surbiton, Surrey, KT6 7NF.
National Anti-Vivisection Society Limited,
(Pet Home-finding Service),

51, Harley Street, London, W1N 1DD.
National Canine Defence League,
10, Seymour Street, London, W1H 5WB.
National Pets Club,
Daily Mirror, 33, Holborn, London, EC1P 1DQ.
Nature Conservancy,
20, Belgrave Square, London, SW1 8PY.
People's Dispensary for Sick Animals,
P.D.S.A. House, South Street, Dorking, Surrey.
Retired Greyhound Trust,
St. Martin's House, 140, Tottenham Court Road, London, W1P 0AS.
Royal College of Veterinary Surgeons,
32, Belgrave Square, London, SW1X 8QP.
Royal Pigeon Racing Association,
The Reddings, Nr. Cheltenham, Glos. GL51 6RN.
Royal Society for the Prevention of Cruelty to Animals,
The Manor House, Horsham, Sussex, RH12 1HG.
Royal Society for the Protection of Birds,
The Lodge, Sandy, Bedfordshire, SG19 2DL.
Scottish Society for the Prevention of Cruelty to Animals,
19, Melville Street, Edinburgh, EH3 7PL, Scotland.
Ulster Society for the Prevention of Cruelty to Animals,
Knockeen, 11, Drumview Road, Lisburn, Co. Antrim,

BT27 6YF.
Universities Federation for Animal Welfare,
    Hamilton Close, South Mimms, Potters Bar, Herts.
Wildfowl Trust,
    Slimbridge, Gloucestershire, GL2 7BT.
World Federation for the Protection of Animals,
    Dreikönigstrasse 37, CH 8002 Zurich, Switzerland.
World Wildlife Fund,
    29, Greville Street, London, EC1N 8AX.

The National Pets Club

The National Pets Club was founded in November 1957 under the sponsorship of the Daily Mirror. It now has a membership of over half a million and is easily the largest Club of its kind in the world.

The aims of the Club are as follows:—

Uniting the millions of people who believe in the humane treatment of animals.

Fostering an interest in both wild and domestic animals, especially among children, and to teach kindness to all living creatures.

Publicising the work of veterinary surgeons and other experts working with animals.

Helping, through the Daily Mirror, in campaigns to stamp out cruelty and neglect.

Advising members on every aspect of animal welfare through the medium of the Club's free postal advisory service.

A fee of 15p covers the cost of enrolment, but membership is run on a non-profit making basis. On joining, each member receives a letter of welcome, a Club badge, a membership card and zoo voucher tickets entitling them to special concessions on entry—or once inside—nine of Britain's top zoos.

The Club operates a 'Silver Paw' scheme and a 'Gold

Paw' scheme. Each member who succeeds in enrolling ten friends receives a silver badge and the title 'Silver Paw Member'. After becoming the holder of a silver badge, they can then go on to achieve a gold badge. To do this, they must enrol a further forty members to the Club, making a total of fifty. As well as receiving a gold badge, they also receive a letter of congratulations and a certificate signed by David Kerr, Editor of the 'Pets Page' which appears in the Daily Mirror every Wednesday.

Although the majority of new members are young people, the Club is nevertheless open to people of all ages and there are no qualifications for membership. Young and old are welcome to join whether they own pets or not. All who join have one bond in common—they are all concerned with the interests of animals.

Whilst we do not solicit donations, it has been found that our members and readers occasionally wish to send us donations for animal welfare. As a result, we have a separate and special fund into which this money is placed and it is used solely to help distressed animals.

A year after the Club began, it introduced a Certificate of Merit. This document is awarded to people who display outstanding kindness and consideration to animals. A number of these certificates have now been awarded to children and adults for exceptional deeds.

Occasionally, the Club presents a 'Silver Medal for Bravery'. This medal is awarded to recognise the achievement of an animal which performed a unique and brave service towards human beings.

The Club offers, free of charge, a wide range of informative leaflets on the care of popular domestic pets. One of the Club's main activities is to give advice to anyone who has a problem involving his pet, or who requires some kind of information connected with the animal world. The law, however, forbids anyone giving veterinary advice by post. The Club's advisory service provides free advice and deals with several hundred personal letters each week.